Praise for Lucy's Va
Approach to Grant Management:

MW00436133

"Lucy's teaching style and presentation of information is very easy to understand. What we valued most is the way she can explain complex legal jargon in a way that is easy for the common person to understand. She presents the facts that an organization needs to know–the parts that are most crucial to the life of grant management at any level."
—J.H., Ada, Oklahoma

"It is obvious that you are very qualified and know your stuff."
—L. F., Lincoln, Nebraska

"This was some of the best training I've ever attended!"
—T. C., Frisco, Texas

"Thank you so much. I received tremendous benefit. I have used the materials several times already to support doing the right thing. It is making grant management a lot easier for me."
—B. P., Denver, Colorado

"You were a delight to work with; thank you!"
—E.R., Portland, Oregon

Here are some of the organizations that have benefited from Lucy's easy-to-understand grant management training:

- Broward County government, Fort Lauderdale, FL
- National Park Service, White Sands, NM
- Virginia Department of Veteran's Services, Roanoke, VA
- Sierra Health Foundation, Sacramento, CA
- College of Emergency Physicians, Irving, TX
- Central New Mexico Community College, Albuquerque, NM
- **And many more...**

Decoding Grant Management

The Ultimate Success Guide
to the Federal
Grant Regulations
in 2 CFR Part 200

by Lucy M. Morgan, CPA

MyFedTrainer.com
Loveland, Colorado

Lucy M. Morgan, CPA / My Fed Trainer, LLC
1635 Foxtrail Drive
Loveland, Colorado 80538
www.MyFedTrainer.com

Ordering Information:
Quantity sales: Special discounts are available on quantity purchases by corporations, associations, and others. For details, contact the "Special Sales Department" at the address above or e-mail Sales@10MinuteMedia.com

Decoding Grant Management, Lucy M. Morgan, 1st edition
ISBN 978-0-9912308-2-2

To each of the grant professionals I have encountered in my travels and those I have not yet met. You are a part of a community of unsung heroes. Your efforts as a grant professional are making the world a better place. Keep making a difference!

–Lucy M. Morgan, CPA

Introduction: My Story
-A Note From Lucy

Are you a grant professional working on federal awards? My story began like that of many of us working in the grant-related professions.

I left my corporate job to make a difference in my community by working with a non-profit organization dedicated to scientific research.

Like many of us, I had no grant-specific training, and yet there I was, smack-dab in the middle of grant management responsible for tracking over $100 million dollars in major project funding from a federal agency.

I accepted that grant management was complicated.

I mean, there are all the rules and regulations…and the jargon…things like MTDC and EVM and IDCR and a host of other fancy terms that only a select few could possibly understand.

(And still today the sad reality is that most people working on federally sponsored projects receive little or no training on how to be a successful grant professional.)

But what I discovered is that it doesn't have to be as complicated as we are led to believe.

(And truthfully, sometimes it seems like it's made as mysterious as possible to exclude people.)

That's how my mission began.

I set out to make resources available so that every grant professional could have the knowledge and skills needed to be successful at grant management.

My hope for you is that this book will help you recognize and avoid the pitfalls that plague many grant recipients while also providing you new opportunities in your career to make the world a better place.

–Lucy

P.S. If this book helps you discover ways to improve grant management and deliver better outcomes to your funding agencies and communities, please let me know.

I am always excited to hear the stories of your challenges and victories.

Send your letters or emails to:

Lucy M. Morgan, CPA

1635 Foxtrail Drive

Loveland CO 80538

Email: LMorgan@MyFedTrainer.com

Website: www.MyFedTrainer.com

Table of Contents

How To Use Decoding Grant Management

This book is designed to make it easy to connect the new grant regulations to your job and career aspirations.

To this end, the book's format has the following elements:

- Section overview of topics
- Relevant content divided into chapters
- Key concepts highlighted at the end of each chapter

While this book is not intended to cover all the rules, regulations, and guidelines unique to your non-federal entity, it does cover the major sections of the federal regulations for grant recipients.

We appreciate your feedback! If you find areas that are unclear, or you believe there is a mistake in the guidance provided, please let us know.

You can email me at LMorgan@MyFedTrainer.com with your comments.

What is 2 CFR Part 200?

This book is based on 2 CFR Part 200 *Uniform Administrative Requirements, Cost Principles, and Audit Requirements for Federal Awards*, popularly referred to as the "OMB Super Circular," or the "Uniform Guidance," or just "UG" for short.

Released December 26, 2013 *and effective December 26, 2014*, the regulations contained in 2 CFR Part 200 supersedes and streamlines the federal grant administration guidance formerly included in OMB Circulars for Administrative

Requirements: 2 CFR Part 215, (A-110) A-102, the Common
Rule, A-89, Cost Principles: 2 CFR Part 225, (A-87) 220, (A-21)
230, (A-122) and Audit Requirements: A-133, and A-50
(Single Audit Act.)

Navigating in Decoding Grant Management

We have added icons exist throughout the study guide to
help you readily identify information.

Overview   Content   Key Concepts

Decoding Grant Management includes twelve sections that
address various concepts in 2 CFR Part 200. This includes
eight sections on the Administrative Requirements for grant
management contained in the Sub-parts A, B, C, and D and
four sections on the Cost Principles in Sub-part E of 2 CFR
Part 200.

 **Section One**

Getting Started with Federal Awards

*R*unning the grant marathon…I picture someone getting ready for a marathon race…training hard… sweating day after day…and finally the big day comes, much like the day you get your first grant! You launch through the starting gate…going fast…the adrenaline rushing…running fast and well.

But then appears the killer hill…or the heavy fog…or a pulled muscle…any of the hundred other things that can happen in a marathon. But on the sidelines there are people ready to help…the water people, the medical team, and most of all, the sideline cheerleaders.

Whether you are just starting the great race of grant management, or have been running along for quite some time, I want you to know that you are making a difference in the lives of people who need help. We are here to cheer you along and support you. Thank you for your commitment to great grant management!

Let's get started…

Overview of Topics

In this section, we'll look at four main areas related to general roles and responsibilities of federal award recipients:

- An overview of the grant process, including how to identify the main types of agreements associated with federal awards
- The purpose of federal administrative requirements
- The applicability of the federal administrative requirements to specific non-federal entities
- The roles and responsibilities of the Office of Management and Budget, the awarding agencies, and the award recipients
- The responsibilities related to subrecipients

At the end of this section, you should recognize and understand the following:

- The main types of agreements associated with federal awards
- The purpose of the federal administrative requirements
- The primary organizations involved with federal administrative requirements
- The primary roles and responsibilities of the Office of Management and Budget, the awarding agency, and the federal award recipient
- The accountability relationship between the federal award recipient and subrecipient

Chapter 1

 # Overview of the Grant Process

ow, just in case you think this is going to be one of those "I walked through the snow five miles to school uphill both ways!" type of story, I have to confess...I had it easy! The grant writers had landed us a multi-year federal award of over a hundred million dollars.

I was fortunate enough to stand on the shoulders of giants, building on the efforts of those who came before me. Life was good! But then everything changed in 2014.

The federal government announced a new set of regulations with an emphasis on performance and accountability. Now both newbies and old hands at grant management have much to learn about how these changes will dramatically change our grant management functions.

Here's an overview of the grant process.

Grant Life Cycle

The grant life cycle officially begins when Congress approves the federal budget for the current fiscal year. At this point, federal agencies receive federal dollars for their use in funding grant programs. Once funded, federal agencies open grant application periods and begin the pre-award process. After the federal agency makes awards, federal award recipients enter a grant management period, when they execute approved projects and programs using federal monies, based on the terms and conditions of the award. At the conclusion of the award period, the federal award recipient and federal awarding agency reconcile financial and reporting activities to close out the grant.

Let's break that down a bit further:

Appropriations Timetable

The grant life cycle starts each year when the US Congress approves the federal budget for the current fiscal year. Upon approval, federal funding for grants becomes available.

The grant life cycle generally starts in February, when the President of the United States releases an annual budget for the following fiscal year. Congressional committees draft budget resolutions that serve as a spending blueprint and set limits on how much each committee can spend. In the early spring, the Congressional Appropriations Committee meets with subcommittees to review priority requests for allocating funds. By late spring, Congress votes on appropriation bills. After the House and Senate Appropriations Committees reconcile the bills, they become the congressional budget for that fiscal year.

The grant life cycle continues in August, when members of Congress visit their districts to listen to the concerns of their constituents. In the summer, Congress typically votes on supplemental appropriation bills. These bills are used when additional money is required beyond the approved budget. In the fall, after the appropriation bills are passed in Congress and reconciled in committee, the congressional budget for the fiscal year is sent to the President. After the President signs the budget, it becomes approved.

Grant Application Period

Once federal funds become available, federal agencies post notices of funding opportunities containing grant information on websites such as www.grants.gov. As applicants submit grant applications, federal agencies first screen the application to ensure completion. Next, a team of federal grant reviewers evaluate the application for merit and risk, covering such areas as technical merit, history of performance, financial stability, business controls, and other issues such as potential conflicts of interest. The cost proposal is also reviewed and verified.

Once a federal agency approves a grant proposal, the federal award recipient receives a notice of the grant. The notice alerts the federal award recipient that an award has been made and how to access federal funding. The notice also contains such items as:

- The terms and conditions of the award
- A grant account number
- The period of performance to accomplish the work
- The dollar amount of the award

The federal government awards grants to non-federal entities planning major projects to benefit specific sectors of the population. Non-federal entities include states, local governments, Indian tribes, institutions of higher education, and non-profit organizations carrying out a federal award as a recipient or subrecipient.

Grant Management Period

The grant life cycle requires quality real-time documentation and timely reporting to effectively manage federal funds and ensure performance goals are achieved. Federal award recipients must stay current with progress reports and other types of required reporting throughout the award period.

Grants are subject to strict government review and must meet performance standards during the award period. Federal award recipients must strictly account for all money spent on grant-funded projects and are subject to detailed audits at least annually. All federal grant monies must be spent on approved projects and any unspent funds must be returned to the United States Treasury.

Federal award recipients must document program goals as approved in the award and complete each phase of the project on time. Federal award recipients must receive approval for most changes to projects as originally approved by the awarding agency. The recipient must demonstrate successful project progress for continued funding.

A federal award recipient may extend the award period by requesting a carryover or a continuation. Federal award recipients should discuss the need for extensions with the federal awarding agency well in advance of the end of the award period.

Extensions may be requested for "cost," which includes additional funds, or "no-cost," which involves a time extension without additional funds. The federal awarding agency may require a supplemental application when a federal award recipient requests additional funds to expand the scope of the project or increase costs. Time extensions require approval by the federal awarding agency.

If a recipient fails to perform as required by the terms and conditions of the grant, penalties will ensue and could include:

- Economic sanctions (which could limit international and domestic trade with your non-federal entity)
- Reimbursement requirements; for example, the awarding agency may require your non-federal entity to return grant funds, pay penalties, go to prison, and/or pay fines

Definitions

Here is an overview of some key definitions for grant recipients getting started with federal awards:

Award

An "award" is financial assistance from the federal government that supports a public purpose. An award includes grants and other types of agreements, which we will cover in more detail in a future section. Perhaps the "award" terminology will make more sense when we look at what an award is not. An award is not technical assistance. Remember, an award must include financial assistance. An award is not a loan, loan guarantee, subsidy, or form of insurance.

Here are some other real-life examples of federally sponsored projects designed to benefit particular sectors of the population.

- Establishing and sustaining Metropolitan Medical Response Centers, also called MMRCs, to support disaster relief
- Providing services to support and retrain displaced workers, such as those in the auto industry
- Lowering infant mortality rates by developing body warmers for pre-mature infants

Recipient or Grantee

"Recipient" or "grantee" refers to a non-federal entity that receives financial assistance directly from a federal agency to carry out a project or program. As used in the federal administrative requirements, a recipient or grantee is a non-federal entity, not an individual that receives financial assistance directly from a federal awarding agency.

Subrecipient

The terms "subrecipient," "subawardee," and "subgrantee" may be used interchangeably in this book. Similar to a recipient, the subrecipient must receive financial assistance in the form of either money or property in lieu of money. Either the recipient or subrecipient makes this award to a subordinate recipient. The term "subrecipient" does not include contractors, also known as "vendors" of goods and services.

Under this regulation, a grant would not include direct payments to individuals. This may be confusing, since the term grant is also commonly used to describe individual grants, such as Pell grants to students.

Contract

The term "contract" can be tricky, because this term can be used both in the "award" world and the "procurement" world. Think of it this way: a procurement contract is generally for the purchase of goods and services, such as a box of pens or servicing the office copier. An award, which may occasionally be called a "contract," must be used for a public purpose, such as researching the effects of pollution or reducing the number of DUI drivers on the road. In other words, the nature of the work performed for the recipient guides how the federal agency views and categorizes the relationship with a contractor or subrecipient.

 **Key Concepts**

• The grant life cycle includes federal budget approval, application period, grant management period, and closeout.

Chapter 2

Purpose of the Regulations

*D*oes the idea of a bunch of new grant regulations make you feel unsettled? (Maybe even a little anxious?) Since the founding of the United States, federal grants have historically been seen as a gift with a few conditions thrown in. The federal government didn't seem to take the concept of performance and accountability too seriously. This is no longer the case.

We have entered a new time in the evolution of grant management, with the OMB Super Circular changes. Some are even calling it "The New Age of Accountability." In the past, making an effort may have been good enough, but now it is performance that matters. And the regulations have a role to play in spelling out everyone's roles and responsibilities.

Purpose

We will look at the purpose of the OMB Super Circular for both federal awarding agencies and recipients. Let's start with the purpose for federal awarding agencies.

For federal awarding agencies, 2 CFR Part 200 gives a consistent and uniform set of rules to be followed by federal awarding agencies. These regulations also provide a yardstick by which federal awarding agencies can measure federal award recipient compliance with the terms and conditions of an award.

For federal award recipients, the new grant regulations provide a consistent and uniform set of rules for assessing a funding opportunity, administering their award, and monitoring and reporting results. For recipients with multiple awards, the regulations provide a level playing field from agency to agency.

Examples of Regulations

Without federal administrative requirements, a non-federal entity would need to guess how to manage federal grant funds. Compliance requirements provide guidelines to ensure that all federal grants are managed consistently.

Consider these examples of federal administrative requirements:

- Obligations that each program operates for a specific purpose (such as the education of children) and all allocated funds should only be used in activities to benefit that purpose
- Cost principles that manage the accounting policies, receipt, expenses, and use of federal funds
- Compliance requirements for the Single Audit Act
- Special award conditions such as Davis-Bacon Act conditions on construction awards
- Earmarking
- Matching requirements regarding cost-sharing
- Procurement methods including support of competition
- Program income guidelines
- Specific reporting requirements
- Prerequisites for subgranting such as risk assessments and monitoring plans

Here is an expansion of some of the areas mentioned above:

Davis-Bacon Act

The Davis-Bacon Act was implemented to require all laborers
employed by a contractor or subcontractor in federally
financed contracts valued in excess of $2,000 to be paid a
wage that is fair for the geographic location of the project.
This provision is also known as "Prevailing Wage Rates."

Earmarking

Certain guidelines define specific goals or objectives the
recipient must achieve in the performance of a federally
funded project. Earmarking is relevant to these guidelines
and requires that a percentage of assistance must (at a
minimum) or may (at a maximum) be used for specific
activities.

Matching

Other regulations govern matching requirements (also
known as cost-sharing). Matching requirements describe the
conditions for using certain contributions to cover a portion
of the program's operations.

Procurement

Grants also come with compliance requirements that the
procurement of goods and services is done in a manner
consistent with federal laws and regulations. Recipients are
required to verify that there is no conflict of interest and to
ensure that contractors are not suspended or debarred, so as
to support open and free competition between contractors.

Program Income

Program income generated from a federally funded program
(such as income for fees for services performed, use of rental
property acquired, or sales of items that originated under the
program) will either be deducted or added to the program
budget as determined by the federal awarding agency.

Reporting

All recipients must submit reports (financial and performance-related) to the federal awarding agency to monitor the use of federal funds. The reports are pre-designed by the federal agency and approved by the OMB, with guidelines and deadlines defined specifically for each program.

Risk Assessment

The responsibilities for the recipient start even before the subaward is made. The OMB Super Circular requires all pass-through entities to perform a risk assessment of the subawardee as part of subaward monitoring prior to subgranting work. Assessing risk can include such things as determining if the subawardee is financially stable and has the ability to effectively implement requirements of the federal award. When needed, the award recipient can impose specific conditions on the subaward to mitigate potential risks.

 **Key Concepts**

- Federal administrative requirements were designed to provide consistency and uniformity for federal agencies and for recipients.

- The OMB Super Circular requirements cover many areas, including financial management, management of federally sponsored programs, cost principles, audit requirements, and other public policy requirements.

Chapter 3

Applicability

Let's face it. No one likes compliance training. Right? No one has compliance-training parties. People don't sign up for "fantasy compliance-training leagues." It's not big in video games. (Although maybe a game where you are crushing regulations could be popular.) It's a problem we all face—how do you keep the nitty-gritty details for the requirements relevant? The two keys for relevance involve making a connection with skill development and real-world application with your job.

Let's explore what happened with federal grant management in the advent of the new Super-Circular.

The OMB Super Circular

Prior to December 26, 2013, federal administrative requirements governing grants administration were tailored to various recipient types. For example, OMB Circular A-102 guided grants administration for state, local, and tribal governments, while 2 CFR Part 215 guided grants administration for non-profits.

In response to recent presidential directives calling for less burdensome and more accountable requirements, the OMB, in partnership with the Council on Financial Assistance Reform (COFAR), overhauled the body of federal regulations governing grants management. As a result, all recipients now follow the same set of federal administrative requirements contained in 2 CFR Part 200 popularly known as the "Super Circular" or the Uniform Guidance.

Effective December 26, 2014, the OMB Super Circular
(2 CFR Chapter I, and Chapter II, Parts 200, 215, 220, 225,
and 230 *Uniform Administrative Requirements, Cost Principles,
and Audit Requirements for Federal Awards*) applies to all
non-federal entities, including states, local governments,
Indian tribes, institutions of higher education, and
non-profit organizations. Commercial enterprises still
follow the Federal Acquisitions Regulations (FAR).

For example, if a local government grants part of the scope
of effort to a non-profit organization, 2 CFR Part 200 would
govern the activities of both the local government and the
non-profit organization.

In addition to the 2 CFR Part 200 requirements, individual
federal agencies and departments may reference additional
agency-specific requirements in the award terms and
conditions.

 **Key Concepts**

• The new grant regulations in 2 CFR Part 200 also known
  as the OMB Super Circular, Uniform Guidance or just
  "UG" provides federal administrative requirements, cost
  principles, and audit requirements for all grant recipients
  and subrecipient organization types.

Chapter 4

Roles and Responsibilities

*J*t's easy to forget why we got into grant management in the first place, given how overwhelming compliance, monitoring, and a mountain of regulations can seem. Federal grants provide the opportunity to do more good in our communities and the world. (And often these objectives couldn't be achieved without the funding support of the federal government.) And it follows that getting more federal grants amplifies the ability to make an even bigger difference.

Let's look at the main players:

Types of Entities Involved with 2 CFR Part 200

The main entities with responsibilities under this regulation are:

- The Office of Management and Budget
- The federal awarding agency
- The award recipient, also known as the non-federal entity

Office of Management and Budget (OMB)

OMB is responsible for issuing guidance for awarding agencies and recipients. OMB integrates their interpretation of legislative and executive policies into the federal administrative requirements. OMB translates the "what" into the" how" for federal awarding agencies and federal award recipients. OMB reviews the various agency regulations to ensure consistency with OMB guidance.

Remember, the main purpose of the federal administrative requirements is consistency and uniformity. OMB is also the organization identified under federal law to grant deviations of federal regulations to federal agencies.

Awarding Agencies

Federal awarding agencies are responsible for implementing the guidance issued by OMB and ensuring that their own agency rules and regulations are compliant with OMB rules. Federal awarding agencies are also responsible for requesting approval for any deviation from OMB regulations.

Federal Award Recipients

Federal award recipients are responsible for complying with all applicable guidance from OMB and awarding agencies. Ignorance of the law is not a defense. Non-federal entities need to know and understand the regulations to which they are subject and also make sure their subrecipients remain in compliance.

 # Key Concepts

- OMB issues guidance governing federal grant administration.

- Federal awarding agencies implement OMB guidance.

- Federal award recipients comply with OMB guidance. and subrecipient organization types.

Chapter 5

🧩 Subaward Responsibilities

●●●

*O*ne of the (many) things I found very confusing when I started working in the world of federal grant management is the way the terms subrecipient, subawardee, contractor, subcontractor, and vendor are bandied about, seemingly interchangeably. It didn't matter if I was talking with my colleagues or federal agency personnel, there always seemed to be lots of confusion around these terms. And I knew making the distinction was important, because there were very different grant compliance and monitoring requirements, depending on which group they were classified with. One of the main responsibilities has to do with monitoring subrecipients.

Subrecipient Monitoring

Federal award recipients have a primary responsibility to ensure subrecipients comply with applicable federal grant management requirements. You may hear this referred to as "subrecipient monitoring" or "subaward monitoring." Let's look at it this way: The recipient is the legal entity to which a federal award is made. Therefore, the recipient is responsible to the awarding agency for how the funds are used and for compliance with all applicable federal regulations.

The subrecipient is the legal entity to which a subaward is made. Therefore, the subrecipient is responsible to the recipient for how the funds are used and for compliance with all applicable federal regulations. When it comes to subaward monitoring, the recipient steps in the shoes of the awarding agency in monitoring subrecipients.

The monitoring responsibilities of the pass-through entity start prior to awarding funds with a risk assessment of the potential subrecipient and then continue throughout the period of the award.

Documentation

The recipient must be able to demonstrate to the federal agency that subrecipients are being monitored for compliance.

This process of documentation starts with the risk assessment done by the pass-through entity to ensure a sufficient monitoring plan is in place and continues throughout the subaward period with adequate documentation to support compliance with 2 CFR Part 200.

 **Key Concepts**

• The recipient has primary responsibility for monitoring their subrecipient(s).

• The recipient must be able to prove that they are conducting monitoring activities.

Section Two

Pre-Award Requirements

*T*he new grant regulations contain over 823 "musts" for federal grant recipients. (The "musts" are described as requirements, while the "shoulds" are described as "best practices.") So how do you know which ones apply to you and your job of managing federal awards?

Let's explore some of the requirements...

Overview of Topics

In this section, you'll explore various topics related to pre-award requirements, including:

- Types of award instruments
- Requirements related to suspension and debarment conditions
- Compliance issues such as special award conditions and policy requirements that may be imposed by funding agencies
- Other contract provisions contained in 2 CFR Part 200

At the end of this section, you should recognize and understand the following:

- Main types of federal awards
- Suspension and debarment requirements contained in 2 CFR Part 200 and related regulations
- A variety of compliance issues including special award conditions
- Various contract provisions that your organization may be subject to as part of 2 CFR Part 200

Chapter 1

 **Types of Awards**

*I*f you want more federal funding, you absolutely want to BE SEEN as the best solution to federal agencies when it comes to their program goals. But being seen can be a scary thing to many of us. And as a result you can consciously (or unconsciously) sabotage your chances. Now, while it's true that getting your first award is usually the hardest ...once you have that, you should be able to increase your funding streams with a little effort.

Let's explore the different ways the federal government spends money and awards funding.

Main Types of Federal Awards

The federal administrative requirements cover three main types of award instruments:

- Grants
- Cooperative Agreements
- Contracts

As a general rule, the awarding agency determines the type of award and the level of their involvement prior to releasing the request for proposal.

Let's look at the differences between these three award types:

Grants and Cooperative Agreements

Both grants and cooperative agreements give federal
financial assistance. Both have a principal aim to accomplish
a public purpose of support or stimulation as authorized by
federal statutes. But a cooperative agreement differs from a
grant in that the awarding agency has far more involvement
in the project or program funded by the cooperative
agreement than it does the project or program funded by a
grant.

Contracts

The area of contracts can be a confusing area for both
agencies and recipients. In many respects an award contract
could look very similar to a procurement contract but be
managed under award rules rather than procurement rules.
When a contract falls under award rules there are more
stringent requirements to follow than when the contract falls
under procurement rules.

Generally, contracts are used by a non-federal entity to
purchase property or services needed to carry out the project
or program under a federal award, such as purchasing a
box of pens or servicing the office copier. But sometimes a
contract is used by a pass-through entity for a subaward
to carry out part of a federal award. And occasionally the
funding agencies will use contracts to carry out what seems
to be for all practical purposes a grant.

When a contract is used for carrying out a public purpose
such as researching the effects of pollution or reducing the
number of DUI drivers on the road, the contract would be
managed under the higher standard of award rules instead
of procurement rules.

Determining which rules to follow boils down to two things:
First, how does the funding agency view the relationship?
Secondly, is the contract providing just goods and services,
or does it anticipate carrying out part of the scope of work
of the award? In other words, the nature of the work and the
funding agencies view of that relationship are most important
in how the work is managed. If you have questions about
whether a contract is administered under the regulations
for grants and cooperative agreements or under federal
procurement law and regulations, please contact your
contracting officer or agency representative.

 **Key Concepts**

- Federal awards are primarily administered under grants or cooperative agreements.

- Federal agencies may use cooperative agreements when they plan substantial involvement between the agency and the awardee to accomplish the project or program.

- Contracts are generally used for the procurement of goods and services.

Chapter 2

Suspension and Debarment

*J*t's every kid's nightmare. That day when a friend says "I don't like you anymore!" This unpleasant situation can also happen to organizations, governmental units, and individuals. It's called "suspension and debarment." It is when the federal government says "I don't like you anymore!" Sometimes, we make up with each other. That's called "suspension." Sometimes, we don't. That's called "debarment." As a grant recipient, you can't let any federal money go to anyone who is suspended or debarred.

This is just one of the requirements related to federal grants.

Definitions

Let's look at the definitions of suspension and debarment:

Suspension

Suspension prevents a person or organization from receiving federal funds. A suspension is a temporary withdrawal of federal support. Usually, this temporary withdrawal is pending some form of corrective action by the award recipient or pending a decision by the agency to terminate the award. A suspension at the award level is different from a suspension at the organizational level.

Debarment

Debarment also prevents a person or organization from receiving federal funds but it is a much more punitive action taken by a federal agency. The debarment prohibits participation in procurement contracts and non-procurement transactions such as grants and cooperative agreements.

Excluded Parties List

Both recipients of federal awards and federal agencies are required to check the excluded parties list system prior to opening bids or awarding work. The excluded parties list system can be checked at the System for Award Management at www.SAM.gov. Non-federal entities and individuals can be excluded from participating in federal awards, subawards, and certain types of contracts if they are suspended, debarred, or otherwise excluded from participating in federal spending.

The Excluded Parties List System (EPLS) is a comprehensive list of individuals and organizations prohibited from participating in federal procurement and non-procurement transactions. This list is maintained and updated continuously by various federal agencies. Both organizations and individuals can be excluded from participation in federal awards, subawards, and certain types of contracts if they are suspended, debarred, or otherwise excluded from participation in federal spending.

Checking the EPLS

Checking the EPLS is easy. Just go to go to the System for Award Management at https://www.sam.gov/portal/public/SAM/. There you will be able to query on both simple searches and advanced searches. For example, you can query on the individual or entity name, the Taxpayer Identification Number, also known as TIN, or other types of criteria.

The federal government requires federal agencies and recipients to check the EPLS at various points during the federal grant life cycle. Federal agencies must check the EPLS for the agency name or principal's name before approving any primary-tier covered transaction, such as a grant, cooperative agreement, or contract. The agency is also required to check lower-tier participants or principals when agency approval is required for the lower-tier transactions. An example of this might be a subaward or other contract that requires agency approval.

Federal recipients, usually through a contracting officer, must check the EPLS to ensure federal monies do not flow to an excluded entity. The contracting officer first checks the EPLS at the opening of bids or receipt of proposals. The contracting officer must check the EPLS again immediately before releasing work or awarding any new work. Recipients need not check the EPLS before issuing payment.

Documenting Suspension and Debarment Compliance

Federal agencies and recipients must document in writing that they checked the EPLS prior to awarding funds or subcontracting work to another entity. Federal law requires the documentation to include when the EPLS was checked and who was searched in the EPLS. Therefore, you must note both the date the EPLS was checked and the criteria used in the query. An easy way to document this is to print the results of the query from your web browser. This will show both the date stamp and the query criteria. Remember, this topic is a favorite of auditors, so put the documentation where it can be easily accessed for both auditors and agency requests.

 **Key Concepts**

- You must check the EPLS before taking any action.

- You must document that you checked the EPLS and keep that documentation easily accessible.

Chapter 3

🧩 Compliance Issues

A recent Inspector General (IG) report highlighted the risk to over $7 billion in undisbursed funds for the High Speed Intercity Passenger Rail (HSIPR) program. (This discretionary grant program supports the creation and expansion of high-speed and inter-city passenger rail networks.) The report delivered a condemning look at the lack of processes and procedures for assessing risk of federal awards.

This is the type of thing that brings special award conditions and other compliance measures to award recipients.

Special Award Conditions

This chapter discusses special conditions covered in the pre-award requirements. Federal agencies may decide to impose special award conditions in accordance with 2 CFR Part 200 for many reasons, including:

- A history of poor performance on awards
- Financial instability in the organization
- Non-compliance with management system standards
- The organization has not conformed to the terms and conditions of a previous award.

High Risk Grantee

The most common reason is that the applicant or grantee is considered high risk. Special award conditions may also be imposed if the subrecipient is deemed high-risk. If the applicant, recipient, or subrecipient is labeled high-risk, several special award conditions could be imposed. These conditions could include:

- Limiting payment of federal funds to a reimbursement-only basis instead of an advance basis
- Requiring performance milestones are met before proceeding to the next phase of the project
- Increasing the number and detail of financial and project reports and monitoring
- Adding more prior-approval requirements in award terms and conditions

Notification

The awarding agency will notify a recipient in writing of any special award conditions placed on it. This written notification must include:

- An explanation of the special award conditions
- The reason for adding special award conditions
- Corrective action needed to resolve any issues and lift the special conditions
- The time frame for completing the corrective action
- Procedure for requesting reconsideration and removal of the special award conditions

Once the conditions that led to the special conditions are corrected, the agency is required to remove the special conditions promptly.

Other Compliance Issues

There are a number of areas in the Uniform Administrative Requirements that the non-federal entity should be aware of, such as:

- Public policy requirements
- Certifications and representations
- Required disclosures
- Risk assessments that must be conducted by federal agencies and pass-through entities

Public Policy Requirements

Federal awards frequently include public policy requirements that are not program-specific. These can be statutory, executive order, other presidential directive, or regulatory requirements that apply by specific reference. Public policy requirements include things like protecting public welfare, protecting the environment, and prohibiting discrimination.

The Resource Conservation and Recovery Act is an example of a regulation that encourages certain types of recycling behavior.

Certifications and Representations

The OMB Super Circular authorizes federal awarding agencies to require annual submissions of certifications and representations from recipients. If the recipient fails to meet a term or condition of the federal grant, the federal awarding agency is authorized under 2 CFR Part 200 to require the recipient to submit certifications and representations more frequently than on an annual basis.

Required Disclosures

The OMB Super Circular also requires the non-federal entity to disclose in writing any potential conflict of interest to the federal awarding agency or pass-through entity. More information about what constitutes a conflict of interest can be found with the applicable federal awarding agency's policy. Another mandatory disclosure requires non-federal entities to disclose in writing and in a timely manner to the federal awarding agency or pass-through entity, all violations of federal criminal law involving fraud, bribery, or gratuity violations potentially affecting the federal award.

Risk Assessments

Both federal agencies and pass-through entities are required to conduct an assessment of risk prior to awarding work. Special conditions can be imposed where necessary to mitigate potential risks of waste, fraud, and abuse before the money is spent.

The framework for this risk assessment can look at such things as:

- Financial stability
- Quality of management systems
- History of performance
- Previous audit reports and findings
- Ability to effectively implement the requirements of the federal award

 **Key Concepts**

- The federal agency can impose special award conditions on grantees for a variety of reasons.

- Applicants and recipients must be notified in writing of the special award conditions.

- Federal awards frequently include public policy requirements that are not program-specific.

Chapter 4

Other Contract Provisions

- -

*M*ore public policy requirements rear their heads in the new OMB Super Circular. New guidance on recycling and use of recovered materials may need to be included. Protection of personally identifiable information (PII) is now part of the electronic age we live in. And yes, you will need to update your contracts provisions in order to be compliant. (But at least the metric system is no longer our preferred system to the extent practicable, so change can be good!)

Let's look at some of those contract provisions…

Contract Provisions

The OMB Super Circular requires the use of numerous contract provisions. You may need to include some of these contract provisions in your contracts that flow down to lower-tier contracts or subawards. It is your responsibility as a federal recipient to understand the requirements and know how they apply to your situation.

In this chapter we will divide the contract provisions between general contract provisions and provisions that apply to construction and research awards. These contract provisions apply to all contracts:

- Equal Employment Opportunity
- Recipient Termination Clause
- Remedies for Breach

- Clean Air and Water
- Energy Efficiency
- Anti-Kickback
- Anti-Lobbying
- Debarment and Suspension
- Recycling

Equal Employment Opportunity

All contracts are subject to the Equal Employment Opportunity contract provision, which ensures equal employment opportunity in the workplace. This executive order makes it illegal for federal contractors and certain subcontractors to discriminate on the basis of race, color, religion, sex, or national origin. This provision also requires federal contractors and subcontractors to take steps to ensure equal employment opportunity in the workplace.

Recipient Termination Clause

A termination clause is required for all contracts valued in excess of $10,000. The termination clause must address termination for cause and for convenience by the non-federal entity, including how the termination will be effected and the terms for settlement of any outstanding amounts.

Remedies for Breach

Contracts for more than the simplified acquisition threshold, which is currently set at $150,000, must address administrative, contractual, or legal remedies in instances where a contractor violates or breaches the contract terms. In this case, the contract provisions must provide for remedies such as sanctions and penalties as appropriate, and a termination clause is required.

Clean Air Act and Clean Water Act

The Clean Air and Water contract provisions must appear in all contracts and subgrants valued at over $150,000. Federal award recipients and subrecipients must agree to comply with all standards, orders, and regulations that apply to these two acts. The Clean Air Act sets standards to regulate air quality, reduce energy waste, and promote energy conservation. The Clean Water Act enforces provisions for restoring and maintaining the chemical, physical, and biological integrity of the nation's water supply. Any violations must be reported to both the federal awarding agency and the regional office of the Environmental Protection Agency (EPA). Recipients must document violations, as well as when and to whom notifications were made.

Energy Efficiency

All contracts must contain energy-efficiency clauses contained in the Energy Policy and Conservation Act. Mandatory standards and policies relating to energy efficiency are contained in the state energy conservation plan issued in compliance with the Act.

Copeland Anti-Kickback Act

The Copeland Anti-Kickback Act enforces consistency in labor standards by protecting employees from being forced to give up any part of the compensation to which they are entitled under contract of employment. This contract provision applies to all contracts and subcontracts over $2,000 for construction or repair. Applicable contracts and subgrants must include the provision and comply with the Act as supplemented by the Department of Labor Regulations 29 CFR Part 3. Federal award recipients must report all suspected or reported violations to the federal awarding agency.

Byrd Anti-Lobbying Amendment

The Byrd Anti-Lobbying Amendment requires contractors applying or bidding for awards over $100,000 to file certification to the tier above them. The contractor must certify that no federal funds were used for lobbying efforts. Lobbying efforts include attempting to influence an employee of any agency. This amendment also requires disclosure of any lobbying that takes place if non-federal funds are used in connection with obtaining a federal award. These disclosures must flow up each tier, all the way to the recipient of the award.

Debarment and Suspension

In addition to checking that the contract or award is not flowing to an excluded party such as a suspended or debarred recipient, contract provisions should contain explicit statements that the funds can't flow to parties who are excluded from receiving federal funds. These statements include the requirement that contractors and recipients are responsible that federal funds do not flow to an excluded party in a lower-tier covered transaction.

Recycling

All contracts must include language explaining that federal agencies and recipients must purchase items made with the highest percentage of recycled materials when the purchase price of the item exceeds $10,000. For all other procurement activities, 2 CFR Part 200 requires a preference for recycled materials. A non-federal entity may need to document its efforts to comply with the provisions.

Construction-Related Contract Provisions

Federal recipients must include these contract provisions in construction-related contracts.

- The Davis-Bacon Act
- Contract Work Hours and Safety Standards Act
- The Right to Inventions for Research Contracts

The Davis-Bacon Act

The Davis-Bacon Act is a federal law that requires paying prevailing wages on certain public works projects. This provision applies to construction contracts over $2,000. Construction-contract provisions subject to Davis-Bacon flow down to both recipients and subrecipients. Federal award recipients must report all suspected or reported violations to the federal awarding agency.

Contract Work Hours and Safety Standards Act

This contract provision is required for all contracts valued in excess of $100,000 that involves the employment of mechanics or laborers. This provision requires all federally assisted contractors and subcontractors to pay laborers and mechanics one and one-half times their basic pay rate for every hour worked beyond a 40-hour work week. The Act also prohibits unsanitary, hazardous, or dangerous work conditions on federally financed or assisted construction projects. This contract provision requires compliance with sections 102 and 107 of the Contract Work Hours and Safety Standards Act as supplemented by Department of Labor Regulations 29 CFR Part 5.

The Right to Inventions for Research Contracts (Bayh-Dole Act)

The Right to Inventions Made under a Contract or Agreement" (also known as the Bayh-Dole Act) provides U.S. universities, small businesses, and nonprofits control of intellectual property and inventions resulting from federal government-funded research. It applies to contracts or agreements for performance of experimental, developmental, or research work. Rights of the federal government and the recipient must be clearly outlined in the document in accordance with 37 CFR Part 401 and any implementing regulations issued by the awarding agencies. The definition of intellectual property covers a wide range of research activities that are partially or completely federally funded.

 **Key Concepts**

- Federal recipients must review required contract provisions and include those that apply to their organization in subgrant and subcontractor agreements.

- Federal recipients must remain compliant with contract provisions.

Section Three

Monitoring
And Reporting

*W*ant to get a bunch of grant professionals excited?
Just bring up the topic of monitoring and reporting.
*I recently shared a humble little article on LinkedIn on
the seven tips for grant management monitoring, and
I was amazed by the response! I felt like people were
leaping up from their desks to get their two cents in for
the top grant management monitoring tips as well!*

It's a big topic full of lots of ideas, myths, and angst!

Overview of Topics

This section discusses financial management systems and focuses on four main areas:

- Reporting requirements for recipients of federal grants and other awards
- Guidelines for internal control in financial management systems
- Standards for documentation of project or program spending
- A list of specific written procedures that a non-federal entity must maintain

At the end of this section, you should recognize and understand the following:

- Reporting requirements of a financial management system
- Components of an effective control system
- Examples of acceptable documentation, with examples of insufficient documentation
- Requirements for written procedures contained in the financial management system requirements

Chapter 1

Reporting Requirements

*ust as the real estate adage says: location, location, location;
results, results, results is the new mantra for award recipients.
More and more, the federal government is asking "What results are
we getting for the money we invest?" No more is it enough just to
spend the last dollar on the last day. Expect more and more pressure
on award recipients to deliver on the promise of RESULTS.*

*Let's get started by looking at how to report those results, and the
role of a financial management system. (Award recipients have
several reporting requirements to be in compliance with 2 CFR Part
200.)*

Measuring Performance

There are a variety of ways that the federal grant regulations
set expectations for grant recipients to measure performance
on federal awards. Here are two common ones:

Relate Financial Data to Performance Accomplishments

Federal award recipients must relate financial information to
performance accomplishments in order to be compliant with
2 CFR Part 200.

Some non-federal entities use Earned Value Management
(EVM) systems to meet this requirement. An EVM system is a
method of tracking financial data, such as project or program

spending, and relating this information to the expected progress on the project or program. For example, if 75% of project funds were spent, but only 50% of the scope of work was completed, this may signal a potential issue to the agency.

Demonstrate Cost Effective Practices

Compliance with the 2 CFR Part 200 also requires tracking unit cost information. Examples of unit cost information could include:

- The cost per person served by a program
- The cost per mile built for a construction project
- The cost per site maintained for a research program

The OMB Super Circular requires recipients to relate financial data and cost information in ways that enable federal awarding agencies to better measure recipient performance. Federal awarding agencies want to assess recipient performance in ways that will help improve program outcomes, share lessons learned, and highlight best practices. To this end, federal awarding agencies are now required to provide recipients with clear performance goals, indicators, and milestones. Additionally, federal awarding agencies must adjust performance reporting frequency and content, not just to monitor recipient progress, but also to readily identify promising practices.

Financial Management

Similar to measuring performance, 2 CFR Part 200 sets guidelines for financial management of the federal award. Here are three foundations of financial management for grant recipients:

Disclosure of Financial Results

Federal recipients must provide accurate, current, and complete disclosure of the financial results of a project or program on a per-award basis. This necessarily entails:

- Maintaining all required disclosures of financial results
- Keeping project or program spending separate from other types of spending
- Keeping financial records and statements up to date

Financial Reporting: Budget vs. Actual

Recipients must be able to track and report on the project or program budget and also report the actual spending against that budget. This may seem obvious, but the reports of actual spending must tie to the financial records and source documentation of the non-federal entity. The source documentation should be reviewed for reliability. Explanations for cost overruns and underruns should be obtained from operational personnel who are responsible for the source data.

Tracking Flow of Funds

Finally, the award recipient must be able to track the source and application of the funds for federally sponsored activities. This means the award recipient must be able to track not only what award the funds were drawn against, but also which award the funds were applied to. For recipients with multiple awards, this requirement addresses reporting not just expenditures, but also how the funds drawn were applied to various awards.

 **Key Concepts**

- The federal agency can impose special award conditions on grantees for a variety of reasons.

- Applicants and recipients must be notified in writing of the special award conditions.

- Federal awards frequently include public policy requirements that are not program-specific.

Chapter 2

Control Guidelines

ou may have heard about it. The new grant regulations are making risk assessment of federal award recipients a requirement for federal agencies prior to awarding any grants.

And the concept of internal controls has moved out of finance and audit supplements where only finance staff monitored this critical aspect of grant management and into the rest of the organization where program managers and staff, as well as senior management now have responsibility for internal controls.

This means more people than ever before are going to need to understand what goes into internal controls.

Effective Control and Accountability

Award recipients must be able to demonstrate effective control and accountability for all cash, property, and other assets. The control requirements for grant management include the use of financial management systems and internal controls, in addition to the reporting requirements we looked at previously. Recipients must also adequately safeguard assets and use them only for authorized purposes as outlined by the terms and conditions of the award.

Demonstrating effective controls includes a broad range of control requirements, such as:

- Compliance
- Record retention
- Asset safeguards
- Written policies and procedures
- Adequate training
- Monitoring
- Segregation of duties
- Protections of assets and information
- Resolving non-compliance

The OMB Super Circular highlights key requirements for effective internal controls:

Compliance

The non-federal entity's financial management systems must be sufficient to permit the preparation of reports required by general and program-specific terms and conditions. The tracking of the federal funds must be detailed enough to assure that federal funds have been used according to the terms and conditions of the award, as well as applicable laws and regulations. A financial-management system should also include documentation that shows compliance with federal statutes and regulations, and the terms and conditions of the federal award.

In addition, states may account for grant funds in a manner consistent with individual state laws and procedures, as long as the fiscal control and accounting procedures are sufficient to meet the federal control requirements.

Record Retention

The financial management systems must provide for record retention and access. This includes such things as:

- Handling requests for records
- Having methods to collect, transmit, and store information safely
- Providing access to records that is consistent with rules and restrictions on public access to records
- Protecting personally identifiable information

Asset Safeguards

The financial management system would demonstrate effective control and accountability by including such things as:

- Adequate safeguards over all assets
- Assurance that assets are used solely for the authorized purposes.

This means assets purchased for a specific project or program would be used solely as authorized by that award.

Written Procedures

Written policies and procedures that demonstrate effective control and accountability in the administration of federal awards can include:

- Procedures that detail the planning and budgeting process
- The process for payment management
- Procedures for determining the allowability of costs for charging the federal award

- A written policy giving specific spending authority
- Written job descriptions illustrating personnel roles and job responsibilities
- Policies and procedures for timekeeping and documenting labor charges

Training

Additionally, effective control and accountability includes making sure employees have adequate training to perform their job duties. Non-federal entities must have in place a training program for new employees and periodic training for existing employees, tailored to their job duties. Training programs that teach proper time and labor allocation to federal awards are highly scrutinized.

Monitoring

Monitoring is an important component of effective control and accountability. Award recipients should demonstrate that they have ongoing monitoring procedures in place to test the effectiveness of existing processes and procedures. Non-federal entities should monitor internal processes and procedures periodically to ensure they work properly.

Federal awarding agencies evaluate and monitor how recipients comply with the terms and conditions of federal awards. Evaluation and monitoring activities can take any form, including site visits by federal monitors to personally evaluate and monitor compliance.

Effective control and accountability recognizes that situations can change. Therefore, a component of good internal controls is to have an appropriate process for modifying processes and procedures as required by changes in conditions. This may include an annual review of existing documentation, and defining a process to follow during emergency situations.

Segregation of Duties

The control requirement for segregation of duties seeks to limit any one person having the responsibility for custody, recordkeeping, and authorization of an asset. This could be demonstrated in many ways, including:

- Review of financial and program reports by someone other than the person who prepared them
- Physical custody of equipment by someone other than the person who can authorize the purchase
- Adjustments to the financial or program records being authorized by someone other than the person recording the change

Protection of Assets and Information

Good controls include protecting both assets and information. This covers areas as wide as maintaining reliable accounting records for fixed assets and inventories. It would be demonstrated by conducting a periodic physical inventory of the assets, comparing the completeness of the property records with the accounting records. It could include preventive measures such as a locked storeroom or server room.

Internal controls also include taking reasonable measures to safeguard protected personally identifiable information and other sensitive information. This can be demonstrated with involvement of the IT department to strengthen cyber security of data and training employees on the policies regarding protection of information and access restrictions. It also includes protecting data from unauthorized disclosures. Recipients must protect all personal information and all information deemed sensitive as required by federal, state and local privacy laws.

Resolving Non-compliance

In the event a federal awarding agency discovers a recipient has failed to comply with a term or condition of a federal grant award, the federal awarding agency could issue a finding of non-compliance. Management must respond and resolve promptly when non-compliance is detected. Actions and corrective actions should be accessed and implemented in light of management reviews, audit findings, and other areas of non-compliance. Management also has a responsibility to follow up on reports of non-compliance and disclose violations of law and conflicts of interest.

Examples of Effective Control and Accountability

Let's look at some real life examples of effective control and accountability:

- Assigning one person as a custodian of assets, such as a stockroom clerk or senior engineer, for a project
- Having a control system for detecting and investigating missing assets
- Performing an annual review and update of policies and procedures
- Regularly reconciling financial accounts, including explanations supporting any account adjustments
- Identifying specific employees as subject-matter experts who ensure compliance with existing policies and procedures
- Maintaining reliable accounting records for fixed assets and inventories
- Conducting a periodic physical inventory of assets and comparing the completeness of property records with accounting records
- Matching reliable property records to financial records and any supporting documentation
- Tracking property records back to a correlating federal award number

- Limiting the risk of asset loss using preventive measures such as locking a storeroom or dividing custody, recordkeeping, and authorization for an asset among several people
- Periodic sampling of expense accounts to determine if unallowable costs are property identified
- Implementing corrective actions in response to management reviews
- Following up on reports of non-compliance with internal controls

When it comes down to it, federal awarding agencies, pass-through entities, and others will assess the adequacy of their financial management systems and internal controls in a variety of ways. To make sure federal funds are being managed prudently, audit reports, on-site reviews, and other information can be requested.

 **Key Concepts**

- Federal grant administration guidelines require that federal recipients demonstrate effective control and accountability in their financial management system.

Chapter 3

 # Documentation Standards

*L*ike zombies rising from the dead, inadequate documentation has a way of returning to haunt you in an alarming way. Want an example? I recently analyzed a case study where the review of administrative and clerical costs resulted in $1.7 million in costs being deemed unallowable! All those moaning sounds are not just the zombies.

Documentation Requirements

According to the OMB Super Circular, the award recipient must be able to support accounting and cost records with adequate source documentation. The documentation should provide the means to verify proper separation of costs among various federal awards and non-Federal spending. The extent of the documentation required is affected by the size and complexity of the non-federal entities and the existing control mechanisms. The nature and type of the documentation needed may also vary, depending on the relationship to specific internal controls.

Examples of Adequacy

Adequate source documentation includes having receipts with sufficient detail to be able to determine:

- What the funds were spent on
- When the spending occurred
- Who made the purchase

Another example includes timecards or other labor reporting completed in a timely manner. A timecard should have sufficient detail to determine:

- What award was worked on
- When the work was done
- Who worked on the award
- When the time was reported

Some specific examples of adequate source documentation might include:

- A purchase request or requisition signed by a manager with direct budgetary responsibility for the project or program being charged for the purchase
- Reports supported by financial records that are reviewed and signed by an appropriate level of management

An example of poor source documentation is a receipt that provides too little detail about the purchase, such as a credit card receipt listing the total amount of purchase, but not the item(s) purchased. Without purchase details, federal recipients cannot ensure that purchases are allowable under the terms and conditions of a federal award.

Other Types of Documentation

Not all examples are related to financial records. Adequate program documentation can also include having a detailed narrative explaining project or program objectives.

Consider some of the specific documentation requirements for information technology departments. The overall control environment requires that IT departments document each major application system in an operations and maintenance manual. Examples of adequate source documentation in an IT systems manual would include:

- The software functions and hardware requirements, how the system operates, and how the databases interact
- Explanations of various system messages and queries that are run or received
- A document listing the restart and notification procedures in the event of a system error or failure
- A list of reports that are routinely generated by the various systems

Likewise purchasing departments have a variety of additional types of documentation to maintain. For example, purchases should be properly authorized in accordance with internal policies and procurement standards. Therefore, purchasing documentation without evidence of proper authorization for the purchase may be considered insufficient source documentation.

It is recommended that the authorization document be included with the rest of the related purchase documentation to support purchasing compliance. Without prior authorization documented in the purchasing records, the non-federal entity may not be able to demonstrate that the purchases were properly authorized before the purchase was made. It is recommended that the authorization document be included with the rest of the related purchasing documentation to support purchasing compliance.

 **Key Concepts**

The key concept here is that adequate source documentation must include the following elements:

- Who spent the funds and who authorized the spending
- What were the funds spent on
- What award should be charged for the spending
- When the spending was authorized and when it was spent

Chapter 4

 # Specific Written Procedures

*A*re you prepared for the day when your program officer asks the grant management team at your organization, "Where are your written procedures?" Ah…well…you know…ouch!

There is a renewed emphasis on this long-standing requirement. And though the requirement hasn't changed much, how you respond to this simple question could be the difference between obtaining more federal funding and stopping the flow of funds to your organization.

Requirements for Written Procedures

The OMB Super Circular outlines written procedure requirements for financial management systems. There are several types of policies and procedures that non-federal entities need to have in writing as grant recipients including:

- Standards of conduct
- Procurement policies
- Payment management
- Reasonableness and allowability of costs

The sufficiency of the written procedures is also a part of evaluating the internal control environment for grant recipients.

Standards of Conduct

Non-federal entities must maintain written standards of conduct. These standards must include provisions covering:

- Conflicts of interest
- Performance of employees involved in the selection, award, and administration of contracts
- The requirement that officers, employees, and agents of the non-federal entity can't solicit or accept gratuities, favors, or anything of monetary value from contractors or parties to subcontracts

However, the organization can set standards for what constitutes a nominal value for an unsolicited gift. The standards of conduct must also provide for disciplinary actions to be taken for any violation of the policy.

Procurement Policies

Non-federal entities must have documented procurement policies. These policies need to include things such as how to:

- Monitor and provide oversight to ensure that contractors perform in accordance with the terms, conditions, and specifications of their contracts
- Avoid purchasing unnecessary or duplicative items
- Award contracts to responsible contractors
- Maintain free and open competition, where practicable
- Maintain sufficient documentation of the procurement history

Payment Management

Recipients of federal awards must have written procedures in place that minimize the time between receiving funds from the U.S. Treasury and paying out funds for program purposes. This guideline encourages the prompt use of grant funds to pay program expenses. The federal government's goal is to encourage funds being drawn that are immediately turned around to pay for program expenses as opposed to sitting in an organizations' bank account.

Cost Principles

Federal recipients must have written procedures in place for applying cost principles. Writing internal procedures for applying cost principles requires understanding and defining four key terms:

- Reasonable
- Allocable
- Allowable
- Unallowable

Best Practices For Written Procedures

A component of creating effective written procedures includes defining terms so the people using the documents understand what is meant along with relevant examples. Here are some illustrations of definitions that you could include with your written procedures for applying cost principles:

Reasonable

The reasonable cost standard means assessing whether the amount of the expenditure exceeds the amount a prudent person would have spent under the same circumstances and at the time the decision was made to purchase the item. This is sometimes called the "prudent person" standard. Note that the decision is measured under the circumstances prevailing at the time the decision was made.

Allocable

"Allocable" means that the costs can be allocated in accordance with the relative benefit received by that activity. Allocability also means that the costs are treated consistently with other costs incurred for the same purpose in like circumstances. The federal government only wants to pay its fair share of expenses compared to others participating in the similar activities in like circumstances.

Allowable

If costs are reasonable and allocable, then an allowability assessment follows. Federal cost principles outline costs that are allowed under the terms and conditions of federal awards. For costs to be allowable, the non-federal entity must apply policies uniformly to all activities, not just federal awards. Allowable costs must also be adequately documented.

Some common examples of allowable costs include:

- Reasonable compensation paid or accrued for employees during the period of the award
- Costs for employee fringe benefits in addition to salary costs
- Materials and supplies purchased for use in performance of the federal award

Unallowability

Conversely, costs not confirmed as reasonable or allocable, and costs explicitly excluded from the list of permissible costs under federal cost principles are likely unallowable.

Some common examples of unallowable costs include:

- Alcohol
- Entertainment costs
- Most advertising, public relations, and marketing costs
- All lobbying costs

 **Key Concepts**

● ●

- Written procedures are required for a variety of purposes, as specified by the grant management regulations.

- The grant recipient needs to review what policies and procedures may be needed to ensure compliance with the OMB 2 CFR Part 200, such as written procedures to ensure that costs charged to federal awards are allowable and to minimize the time between receiving federal funds and paying vendors.

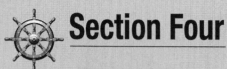 **Section Four**

Payment
Management
Standards

*m*istakes around payment management are so
common that the Federal Audit Clearinghouse
uses standard codes for reporting them when audit data
is reported. While it typically affects a very small group
of people and organizations, it is one auditors LOVE to
look for.

Overview of Topics

In this section, we will look at four main areas:

- The control requirements related to payment management standards for recipients
- Payment methods that are used by agencies to remit federal funds to recipients
- Types of payments that may be included in the cash request to your funding agency
- A list of requirements specific to the type of accounts where the funds can be placed

At the end of this section, you should recognize and understand the following:

- Control requirements for payment management
- Types of payment methods for obtaining federal funds
- Items that may be included in payment requests from the funding agency
- Requirements to receive advanced funds from federal agencies

Chapter 1

Control Requirements

* * *

*W*hen organizations get federal funds advanced to them, sometimes they take the money too soon. Here's an extreme example to illustrate the point:

Let's say that you draw $1 million in advances, but you don't actually pay the contractors until six months later. This would be a violation of the grant management regulations because you're taking those advances too soon. You have a duty to make sure that you're only taking what you need to pay your immediate cash requirements.

Types of Control Requirements

There awill discuss four main areas in this chapter on control requirements:

- Drawing down funds for immediate cash needs
- Minimizing the time from transfer of funds to subsequent payment for program costs
- The need to have specific written procedures in place
- The reporting requirements to meet the financial management systems standards with regard to payment management

Immediate Cash Requirements

Recipients must limit their funding requests to the minimum amount needed to support the program or project. The funding amount must be used to carry out only the purpose of the approved program or project. This requirement means funds may not be drawn to support unrelated work, or in excess of actual funding needs. Funding requests must be timed to coincide with actual immediate cash needs. This requirement is sometimes called the "three-day rule", but this term is a bit of a misnomer, as the requirements use the term "immediate," without specifying a time span.

Note that this requirement should not be confused with the "three-day draw-down window," which applies to certain types of payments to state and local governments.

Time to Transfer

Recipients must have a process that minimizes the time between receiving cash advances from the U.S. Treasury and the actual disbursement of funds by the recipient for program or project costs. Recipients must make timely payments to contractors under existing contract provisions. This time frame should be as short a turnaround as is administratively feasible. Think of administratively feasible as what a prudent person would do in similar circumstances.

Written Procedures

It is not enough to just have a process for minimizing the actual time between receipt of the funds from the U.S. Treasury and subsequent disbursement by the recipient. You must also put that process into a written procedure. Personnel with responsibilities in this area should also know where the written procedure is published for your non-federal entity.

Reporting Requirements

This control requirement focuses on the reporting requirements to meet the financial management system standards. A component of payment management is the ability to track the inflows and outflows of federal funds attributable to specific federal awards.

Recipients must have the ability to track the source and application of funds received and spent on federally sponsored activities. Additionally, recipients must be able to report on which award funds were received and what they were spent on.

Definitions

The reporting requirements also state that the recipient's reports must contain information on the following items related to federal awards:

- Authorization of federal funds
- Obligations in support of projects and programs
- Unobligated balances
- Outlays of federal funds

Let's look at some of this terminology:

Authorizations

Authorizations are simply the total amount of federal funds obligated, which is the amount of the federal award the federal government has authorized for use by the recipient. Authorizations may include carryover from prior funding periods if authorized by the agency. Note that carryover is only allowed when permitted by agency regulations or agency implementing instructions.

Obligations

Obligations are the amount of orders placed for contracts and grants. Obligations are for services received and similar transactions that occur during a specific period, and require payment from the recipient to settle the obligation.

Unobligated Balances

Unobligated balances can be expressed as a mathematical formula where the cumulative obligations are subtracted from the cumulative funds authorized by the federal awarding agency. The result is unobligated balances. Think of unobligated balances as the remaining part of the award that has not been spoken for yet.

Outlays

Outlays are also called expenditures. Outlays are charges made to the project or program and are reported on either a cash basis or an accrual basis.

 # Key Concepts

• •

- The recipient must comply with payment management standards regarding written procedures, reporting, and tracking of draw-downs and expenditures.

- The recipient must have both written procedures and an actual process that limits the *cash request* to support only immediate cash needs for the project or program.

- The recipient must also have both written procedures and an actual process that *minimizes the time between drawing funds* and *making payment* to support the project or program.

Chapter 2

Payment Methods

I have to tell you this flat out: having federal funds advanced to you is SWEET! No worries about making payroll and paying this week's bills. It's not available to every organization, but if you can structure your grant this way, your finance and accounting folks will LOVE it!

Methods for Receiving Federal Funds

Federal award monies may be disbursed either by a cash advance or through funds reimbursement:

Cash Advance

Cash advance is the preferred method if the recipient maintains or demonstrates the willingness to maintain financial management system standards. If possible, advances for multiple federal awards should be consolidated to cover anticipated cash needs. An example of when consolidation would not be possible is when multiple agencies or multiple payment methods are used by the federal awarding agencies. Recipients are authorized to request funds at least monthly when electronic funds are not used, and as often as they like when electronic transfers are used.

Reimbursement of Funds

Reimbursement of funds is the preferred method when the recipient cannot demonstrate the ability or the willingness to maintain the financial management system standards, or when the recipient requests reimbursement. When the reimbursement method is used, the federal agency is required to make reimbursement payments within thirty days of the receipt of the invoice. This assumes that the billing is proper and includes allowable costs. Similar to the advance method, reimbursements may be requested at least monthly.

When available, the non-federal entity must first use funds from things like program income, contract settlements, audit recoveries, rebates, refunds and interest earned before requesting additional funds from the federal government.

 **Key Concepts**

- The advance method is the preferred method for accessing federal award monies.

- The reimbursement method will be used if the recipient cannot meet the compliance requirements in the financial management standards.

Chapter 3

Payment Types

*Y*ale University pays $7.6 million to settle allegations related to indirect charge inclusion and cost transfers. Duke University repays $1.7 million because of inclusion of direct unallowable costs as well as inadequate policies and processes concerning monitoring the compliance of all federal projects at the university.

These are just a couple of examples of what can happen when unallowable costs are paid with federal grant funds. Would you know an unallowable cost if you saw one? Could your organization accidentally request payment for items that can't be charged to a federal award?

Types of Allowable Costs

Two types of costs can be included in requests for cash advance or reimbursement:

- Costs for allowable direct program or project costs
- Costs to cover the federal government's proportionate share of any allowable indirect costs

Consider these definitions for direct and indirect costs:

Direct Costs

Direct costs are costs that can be attributed to a particular final cost objective, such as a federally funded project or program. Direct costs can also be attributed to non-federally funded activities.

Direct costs can be classified as either allowable or unallowable. For example, working on a private foundation grant may be an example of direct costs, but would not be allowable to charge the federal government. Only allowable direct costs would be charged to a federal award.

Indirect Costs

Indirect costs are incurred for joint or common objectives that are not easily identified with a particular final cost objective, such as a project or program. Indirect costs are frequently thought of as support or administrative services. Examples of indirect costs include accounting, human resources, and purchasing departments.

Note: institutions of higher education may use the term "F & A" costs instead of indirect costs. F & A is the acronym for "facilities and administrative" costs.

Similar to direct costs, indirect costs could have an unallowable cost component. For example, if lobbying costs are included in the organization's indirect costs, those types of costs would be excluded from the portion of indirect costs being covered by the federal award.

 **Key Concepts**

• The request for funds can include both allowable direct costs and the proportionate share of allowable indirect costs.

Chapter 4

Specific Fund Requirements

It's official. You are getting the money to pay for your grant. Things are starting to happen. Maybe many things are happening. Multiple awards, lots of program work, hiring people, and work is getting busy! The last thing you may be thinking of is a separate bank account.

The good news is that federal agencies may not require grant recipients to keep separate bank accounts for federal funds unless specified in a federal-state agreement. Seem too good to be true? It could be if you don't track the money in a certain way.

Requirements for Funds

The payment management standards in 2 CFR Part 200 specifies such fund requirements as:

- Whether the funds must be separated
- Where the funds must be located
- What is required for interest-bearing accounts

Separation of Funds

Federal agencies may not require recipients to keep a separate account for federal funds, with few exceptions. Recipients must be able to account for the receipt, obligation, and expenditure of federal funds in a co-mingled account. This means that even though all the various funds come into the same account, the recipient must be able to report on the use of the funds as if the accounts were separate.

Location of Funds

The payment management standards state that federal grant advances shall be deposited in an insured account whenever possible. The FDIC insurance limits may be insufficient to cover the total fund balances. You can view FDIC insurance limits at www.fdic.gov. The insurance limit for organizations is usually lower than the limits for individuals.

It is important to document, and it may be necessary to disclose, the amount of funds exceeding the current insurable limit on your account. This disclosure would generally be part of the audited financial statement disclosures for your non-federal entity.

Interest Bearing Accounts

Recipients are generally required to maintain advances of federal funds in interest-bearing accounts, with some exceptions.

The first exception is for recipients receiving less than $120,000 in federal awards annually. The next exception on the interest-bearing account requirement is when the expected interest in the best available account would not exceed $500 per year. In both instances, federal law does not require advances of federal funds to be held in an interest-bearing account.

Another exception to the interest-bearing account requirement is if the bank requires an average or minimum balance so high that it would not be feasible for the recipient to maintain that type of account. Remember, there is also a requirement addressing drawing cash advances only for immediate needs. Meeting a minimum balance to get an interest-bearing account would not qualify as an immediate need.

Additionally, if a foreign government or banking system prohibits interest-bearing accounts, then this would be an exception to the general rule.

If the interest earned on federal money held in an interest-bearing account is $500 or less per year, the interest may be retained by the recipient to cover administrative expenses. If the interest earned is more than $500, the amount over $500 must be remitted to the Department of Health and Human Services Payment Management System annually. The excess interest is not returned to the awarding agency, nor is it retained by the recipient.

 # Key Concepts

- Federal funds do not have to be held in separate bank accounts as long as the source and use of the specific award funds can be determined.

- Advanced federal funds must be kept in an insured account when possible.

- Payment advances should be maintained in an interest-bearing account, although there are a few exceptions.

- Any interest earned in excess of $500 must be remitted to the Department of Health and Human Services.

78

 **Section Five**

Other Financial and Program Topics

In the new grant regulations in 2 CFR Part 200, the OMB has embraced new approaches, which include innovative and cost-effective ways to improve the results of grant making and grant management processes.

This rethinking of the grant process includes experiments that focus on accountability through performance more than through compliance. An objective of the new guidance is to redirect federal dollars toward organizations with a proven track record of accomplishing program objectives. These new initiatives encourage redirection of grant funds to organizations with a strong track record of program effectiveness.

Overview of Topics

In this section, we will look at four main areas related to financial and program management:

- The requirements for revising budgets and program plans
- The standards for cost-sharing and program income
- Audit standards for recipients of federal awards
- Insurance and bonding topics

At the end of this section, you should recognize and understand the following:

- When budget and program plan changes require prior approval
- Acceptable criteria to include items in cost-sharing funds
- Which audit standards your non-federal entity is subject to
- When insurance and bonding may be required for your award

Chapter 1

 # Revision of Budget and Program Plans

I like to believe that it is rare that a grantee would intentionally misuse funds. However, without proper planning and documentation, an organization places itself at risk for misuse of funds. Prevention of these undesirable outcomes starts at the beginning of the grant application and writing process. Organizations that carefully construct and review the budget delivered to the grantor, making certain that the budget is adequate and realistic in terms of meeting grant requirements; reduce the risk of misuse of federal funds.

But what do you do when things change after the budget is sent to your funding agency?

Revisions

Program plan and budget changes may require the prior approval of the funding agency. The specific requirements can vary, depending on the type of the award, and can be dependent on specific agency rules as well. The instances that follow usually require prior approval from the funding agency:

- Deviations from budget and program plans
- Revisions to program plans and budgets
- Changes to the scope or objectives of the program or project

- Need for additional federal funds to complete the program or project
- Situations listed in the Cost Principles requiring prior approval from the funding agency

It is important that recipients fully understand situations requiring prior approval or they risk having costs disallowed.

Documentation of Prior Approval

In order for prior approvals (pre-approvals) to be effective, they must:

- Be in written form
- Come from an authorized official at the funding agency

Recipients should keep a record of the prior approval for future reference.

Specific Prior Approval Situations

A discussion of situations requiring prior approval follows for each of these areas:

- Non-construction awards
- Construction awards
- Research awards
- Areas that are at the discretion of the federal awarding agency

Non-Construction Awards

In addition to the general requirements for prior approval, non-construction awards also require prior approval when:

- Making changes to key personnel on the project or program
- The approved project director or principal investigator anticipates a reduction in time allocated to the project. This reduction could be an absence exceeding three months or at least a 25% reduction in the time devoted to the project.
- Transferring funds between direct and indirect cost budgets
- Changes in the amount of cost-sharing or matching provided by the recipient.
- Transferring any funds budgeted for participant support costs to some other expense category. Participant support costs are commonly referred to as "training allowances" and include such expenses as stipends, travel costs, and registration fees paid to participants in connection with conferences or training projects
- Making subawards or subcontracts of program work not identified in the original award application or addressed by the terms and conditions of the award

Note that purchases of general types of support services, supplies, materials, or equipment are generally not considered contracting or transferring program work.

The Cost Principles provides additional instances requiring prior approval.

The awarding agency has authority to waive some of the requirements for prior approval contained in the Cost Principles for your non-federal entity.

Construction Awards

If the federal award includes both construction and non-construction funds, recipients may not transfer the budget or funds between construction and non-construction activities without prior approval of the funding agency.

Research Awards

Research awards must follow the general requirements for prior approval in addition to the requirements for construction or non-construction awards, as applicable. However, research awards are allowed a special exception to the prior approval requirements in one special area:

- Research awards can receive a one-time no-cost extension without prior approval unless prohibited by the terms and conditions of the award or unless other exceptions apply.

Agency Discretion

The OMB Super Circular permits federal awarding agencies to waive certain cost and administrative requirements related to timing of award expenditures and transferring funds between spending categories. Some examples of items for which the federal awarding agency may waive prior approval include:

- Pre-award costs incurred up to ninety calendar days ahead of the award start date. The recipient is still on the hook for the pre-spending if the non-federal entity doesn't receive the award or if the award is less than anticipated.
- Carrying forward unobligated balances to subsequent funding periods

- Restricting the transfer of funds and budgets between direct cost categories. Federal agencies may restrict transfers if they equal more than 10% of the total budget and the total budget exceeds the current Simplified Acquisition Threshold of $150,000.

 **Key Concepts**

Prior approval is generally required for:

- Change in the scope of the program or project work
- Change in the objectives of the program or project
- Changes in the amount of federal funds needed to complete the project
- Items listed in 2 CFR Part 200 that require prior approval of the funding agency

The grant regulations do allow funding agencies some authority to waive certain prior approval requirements for grant recipients.

Chapter 2

Cost Sharing and Program Income

More and more federal grants require that a cost-sharing or matching portion be contributed by the grant recipient. The regulations regarding what can be included in cost-sharing funds can be complicated, especially when property or services are donated as part of the cost sharing. This area gets a lot of scrutiny from auditors and agencies alike.

Let's explore the specifics in more detail…

Cost Sharing

Cost sharing, which is also called matching, represents the portion of a project or program not funded by the federal government. Cost sharing can include both cash and in-kind contributions.

When you use in-kind contributions for cost sharing the costs must be:

- Verifiable from the recipient's financial records
- Exclusive to a specific award (You cannot count the same cost-sharing items on multiple awards.)
- Both necessary and reasonable for use by the project or program
- Related to the objectives of the program or project
- Allowable under the Cost Principles for your non-federal entity

There may be other provisions in the cost-sharing regulations that your non-federal entity may need to conform to as well.

What Can Be Included?

Recipients may contribute both services and property for their share of the match. Property can include both real property, such as a building, and personal property, such as office supplies. Recipient contributions must be valued at fair market value. Employee labor contributed by a recipient can include reasonable, allowable, and allocable fringe-benefit costs.

The fair market value of volunteer services may also be included in the value of cost sharing, provided the volunteer services are an integral and necessary part of the project or program. If fringe benefits are paid on behalf of volunteers, the costs that are reasonable, allowable, and allocable may be included in the value of the cost sharing as well. The labor rates used in calculating the cost sharing for either the volunteer services or the recipient's employee services must be consistent with those paid in the labor market for similar work. If a recipient's employees are working in their typical work duties, the rate should be the same as what they are normally paid. If a recipient's employees are not working in their typical duties, the rate used for cost sharing must be consistent with similar work actually performed in the market. For example, if a volunteer who is also an attorney sweeps floors at the recipient's offices, the recipient may only value the volunteer services at the fair market value of someone sweeping the floor and not at the going rate for an attorney.

Cost sharing may also include donated supplies, such as expendable equipment, materials, and office supplies. The value of the donations must be reasonable and can't exceed the fair market value of the items at the time the donation was made. The value at the time of donation could be different than what the donor paid for the items when purchased.

For donated property such as equipment, buildings, and land, where the title passes to the recipient, the value of the cost sharing is different, based on the purpose of the award. If the purpose of the award is to acquire equipment, buildings, and land, then the total value of the donated property at the time of the donation may be included in the cost-sharing amount. If the purpose of the award is to support activities that may use the donated property rather than to acquire property, then normally only depreciation or use charges may be included in the cost sharing. For example, if a building was donated to host a clinic, the cost-sharing value normally would only be the depreciation charges on the building. However, if cost sharing is required to support expansion of a national forest, the donated land could be valued at fair market value for the purpose of cost sharing.

How Are Donations Valued?

For donated land and buildings, the cost-sharing value can't exceed the appraised fair market value at the time of donation. For equipment, the value of the cost sharing can't exceed the fair market value of the equipment at the time of the donation, for equipment of similar age and condition. What the donor paid for the property is generally not relevant to the cost-sharing value.

Donated space can't be valued over the fair rental value of comparable space. The value of the donated space must be established by an independent appraisal of comparable space in a privately owned building in the same locale. This area of valuation has had a lot of scrutiny, so be prepared to document the valuation for cost sharing as required.

Equipment that is loaned to the recipient cannot be valued for the purpose of cost sharing at more than the fair rental value of similar equipment.

Documentation

Federal agencies critically review cost-sharing documentation, so be prepared for additional scrutiny in this area. For cost sharing, the recipient must document the basis for determining the value of:

- Personal services
- Materials
- Equipment
- Buildings
- Land

The purpose of the documentation is to substantiate the valuation was fair, given market condition and use. For example, when feasible, the value of volunteer services should be supported by the same methods used by the recipient for their own employees.

Program Income

Program income is income generated by an activity funded by a federal award. Recipients must track all program income and account for it to the awarding agency. Some examples of program income include:

- Rental fees for property acquired under federally funded programs and projects
- Fees for services performed when the services are paid for under a federal award
- License fees or royalties on patents and copyrights generated as a direct result of federally funded activities

Methods for Program Income

The treatment of program income depends on the funding agency and the award terms and conditions. Federal awarding agencies use three primary methods for addressing program income:

- The additive method—program income is added to the total funds for the project or programs to further the objectives of the award.
- The deductive method—program income is deducted from the program costs to determine net allowable costs.
- As cost sharing or a match—program income is used to finance the non-federal share of the project or program.

 **Key Concepts**

- In-kind contributions of services and property may be included in the cost-sharing requirements if the contribution is valued fairly.

- The valuation must be sufficiently documented and the use of the contributed services or property must be integral to achieving the project or program objectives.

- Program income is generated as a direct result of an activity funded by a federal award.

- Non-federal entities must account to federal awarding agencies for program income.

- The method for accounting for program income depends on the specific awarding agency and the award terms and conditions.

Chapter 3

Audit Standards

In a move that seems counterintuitive to greater oversight, the single audit threshold has been raised to $750,000 in federal awards. At the same time, federal agencies will expand their use of audit resolution methods to reduce repeated audit findings. The federal government has a renewed focus on reducing and resolving audit findings with non-federal entities receiving federal funds.

Audit Threshold

Any non-federal entity that spends $750,000 or more in federal award funds during the non-federal entity's fiscal year must have a single or program-specific audit completed for that fiscal year. This provision does not apply to for-profit subrecipients.

This increase in the threshold from $500,000 for the Single Audit Act is part of the new OMB Super Circular and takes effect in fiscal years after December 26, 2014.

Non-federal entities that spend less than $750,000 in federal award funds for the non-federal entity's fiscal year are exempt from single or program-specific audit requirements, but could still be subject to other types of audit activities. For example, such non-federal entities may still be subject to an Inspectors General audit or other federal agency audit as deemed necessary to carry out a federal agency's responsibilities under federal statute.

Compliance Supplement

The specifics for auditors of federal grant recipients are contained primarily in the new Compliance Supplement to 2 CFR Part 200. Note that these guidelines replace the guidance formerly contained in A-133 audit requirements.

 **Key Concepts**

- Effective for fiscal years beginning after December 26, 2014, non-federal entities must spend over $750,000 in aggregated federal funds during the non-federal entity's fiscal year to be subject to a single audit for that fiscal year.

- While non-federal entities that spend less than $750,000 in aggregated federal funds during a given fiscal year are relieved of single or program-specific audits for that fiscal year, they could still be subject to audit activities by other federal agencies.

Chapter 4

Insurance and Bonding Topics

Insurance and bonding can be more complex than you may realize, when it comes to the requirements around property purchased with federal funds. Making assumptions about whether to insure or not insure can be costly for your organization. When doubt, read your award terms and conditions to see what is needed.

Agency Requirements

The non-federal entity that spends $750,000 or more in fefederal awarding agency may require additional insurance or bonding if the federal government guarantees or insures the repayment of money borrowed by the recipient. The awarding agency may also require additional insurance or bonding if the amount of insurance carried by the recipient is judged to not be adequate to protect the interests of the federal government.

Insurance Requirements

Insurance coverage for property and equipment purchased with federal funds should be equivalent to coverage the non-federal entity carries on the non-federally funded purchases consistent with sound business practices. However, when the federal government retains title to the property or equipment, the terms and conditions of the award will govern the insurance requirements. In most cases, property owned by the federal government is not insured separately by the non-federal entity.

 **Key Concepts**

- The funding agency, at its discretion, can require additional insurance or bonding as it sees fit to protect the federal government's interests.

 **Section Six**

Property Standards

*P*roperty purchased with federal funds seems to attract grant management mistakes. Sometimes organizations will buy equipment and in short order nobody really knows where it is. Or as an award recipient, you may not know you have reporting and physical inventory requirements. And like the kid who moves home to live in your basement, property tracking needs to be supported for many years past what you expected when you signed up for your award.

Overview of Topics

In this section, we will look at four main areas related to property standards:

- The various types of property covered in the standards
- The various ways that title to property purchased with federal funds can be held
- The requirements for care and use of property
- Specific requirements related to disposing of property obtained during the award period

At the end of this section, you should recognize and understand the following:

- Types of property covered in 2 CFR Part 200 Property Standards
- Different ways that property can be titled on federal awards
- Requirements for care and use of property purchased with federal funds
- Specific requirements for disposing of property purchased during the award period

Chapter 1

 # Types of Property

George Orwell observed that when you control the language, you control the people. The same could be said about defining property management responsibilities for award recipients. The definitions of property as real, personal and expendable control how you track the property and what happens when you are done with it. Let's get a common understanding of the language around different types of property that you may encounter on your award.

Definitions

The Property Standards part of 2 CFR Part 200 covers four types of property:

- Real property
- Equipment
- Supplies and other forms of expendable property
- Intangible property

"Expendable" means property that can be consumed.

Real Property

Real property includes land and the improvements on the land, such as a parking lot or landscaping. Real property also includes any structures on the land, such as buildings. Items such as movable machinery and equipment do not fit the definition of real property. For example, a furnace installed in a building would be part of the real property, but a space heater would not.

Equipment

Equipment includes tangible personal property with a physical presence, such as a drill press. As of 2014, the federal government also classifies information technology systems and software as equipment. Compare this to intangible property, which lacks a physical presence, such as a copyright. Personal property doesn't necessarily mean for personal use. The term "personal" simply differentiates property from real property.

Personal property must have a useful life of more than a year and an acquisition cost of more than $5,000 per unit in order to be classified as equipment. If the property has a value of more than $5,000, but doesn't have a useful life of at least a year, it would not be classified as equipment. Federal recipients with an internal equipment policy that defines equipment as less than the $5,000 federal threshold must use the same definition for federal purposes at the lower amount. Federal recipients that define equipment consistent with the federal definition do not have this issue.

Supplies and Other Expendables

"Supplies and other expendables" is the catchall category for personal property that fails to meet the definition of equipment or intangible property. Examples of supplies and other expendables include computers and computer accessories with a purchase price less than $5,000, office supplies, and packing materials, such as bubble wrap or pallets.

Intangible Property

"Intangible property" is personal property lacking a tangible or physical presence. Examples of intangible property include lease agreements and software. Intangible property also includes copyrights, patents, and other intellectual property, only if such property was acquired during the grant award period. Intellectual property developed or generated during a grant award period is not classified as intangible property and receives different treatment under federal grant guidelines.

 **Key Concepts**

- Real property includes land and improvements.

- Equipment includes tangible personal property with a useful life of more than one year and a cost of more than $5,000, or the non-federal entity's capitalization limit, whichever is lower.

- The supplies category is the catchall category for personal property that fails to meet the definition of equipment.

- Intangible property includes items lacking a physical presence. Intellectual property is federally defined as intangible property only if it was acquired and not created during the grant award period.

Chapter 2
Property Title

*M*any a grant recipient has the mistaken belief that property
purchased with federal funds is just like any other property. In
actuality, real property and how the property is titled will have an
impact on insurance requirements, disposal procedures in the future,
and more. . .

Federally-Owned Property

Property purchased with federal funds can either be titled
as either federally-owned or recipient-owned. Let's look as
some of the nuances of the ways property can be titled:

Real Property

Generally, real property acquired with federal award funds
is not titled to the federal government. However, specific
statutes can require that the title to real property "vest," or
stay, with the federal government.

Equipment

Recipients must maintain a record of all federally owned and
federally funded equipment. These records must include
a description of the property, identifying numbers, source
of the property, title holder, acquisition date, property cost,
and percentage of federal participation in the property cost,
location, condition, use, and disposition data for the property.
The recipient must also specifically and clearly identify
federally owned property, such as by affixing a "federal
government owned" sticker to federally owned property.
Recipients must conduct a physical inventory of all federally

owned and federally funded equipment at least once every
two years to update equipment records.

Supplies

Supplies and other expendables are generally not titled or
owned by the federal government, but the recipient must
still ensure that these items are used only for their intended
federal purpose.

Intangible Property

Like supplies, intangible property is not usually titled with
the federal government. The federal awarding agency,
however, may retain nonexclusive and irrevocable rights
to use the intangible property for federal purposes without
having to pay royalties. The federal government can also
authorize others to use intangible property under the same
royalty-free rights.

Recipient-Owned Property

Recipient-owned property, also known as "exempt"
property, is property titled to the recipient. The agency
must have statutory authority to grant ownership to the
recipient. Even when ownership is granted to the recipient,
the recipient may have ongoing responsibilities to the federal
government such as reporting and tracking requirements,
controlling the use of the property, and seeking instructions
prior to disposing of the property.

Real Property

The recipient must also use property titled to it only for the
purpose the federal awarding agency has authorized. The
recipient must get the written permission of the federal
awarding agency to use the real property on other federally
sponsored projects or programs.

Equipment

When the recipient has title to equipment purchased with federal funds, it is with the condition that the equipment will be used only by the program or project for which it was acquired. The federal awarding agency can instruct the recipient to move the equipment to a different project that won't interfere with the original project objectives. The recipient also cannot put liens or otherwise encumber the equipment without the federal awarding agency's approval.

The recipient is also prohibited from providing services to non-federal entities using the equipment at a cost lower than a private company would offer similar services, unless the activity is specifically authorized by federal statute. So, if the cost of equipment is borne by the federal government, the recipient could have an unfair advantage over a private company that has to purchase its own equipment.

Supplies

Supplies and other expendables are generally owned by the recipient. Like equipment, the recipient can't provide services to non-federal entities using supplies and other expendables at a cost lower than a private company would offer similar services, unless the activity is specifically authorized by federal statute. The recipient must also ensure that property is used for the intended federal purpose.

Intangible Property

The recipient is free to copyright work developed during the award period. The recipient must follow federal regulations related to patents and inventions. These regulations generally do allow certain recipients to apply for patents on inventions developed during an award period. The recipient is also required to comply with the Freedom of Information Act (FOIA) and may have to provide documents including development information upon request.

Other Issues

Three additional areas merit discussion on the topic of equipment titling:

- The equipment inventory listing
- The requirement for an equipment physical inventory
- The types of items that must be included in the detailed equipment records

Inventory Listing

For all federally owned property in the custody of the recipient, an annual inventory listing must be sent to the federal government. This requirement also states that the recipient must restore federally owned property to the federal awarding agency at the conclusion of the federal award or when the property is no longer needed by the activity. Note that this requirement says federally owned property, and not just equipment.

Physical Inventory

A physical inventory is required every two years for federally owned equipment. The inventory process must reconcile the equipment records with the accounting records. The recipient has a duty to investigate any differences between the physical inventory of the equipment, the equipment records, and the financial records. Note that this requirement says federally owned equipment and not property. The recipient is required to both verify and document the existence of the federally owned equipment, how the equipment is currently used, and any continued need for the federally owned equipment.

Equipment Records

Equipment records for both federally owned and recipient-owned property must include:

- Whether the title is vested with the federal government or the recipient
- Identification number of the award that funded the purchase of the equipment
- A description of the equipment
- Acquisition source, such as the company, where the equipment was purchased
- Equipment identification number, such as a serial number or model number, so specific equipment can be tied back to the original purchase
- Acquisition date
- Total cost and per-unit cost, if different
- Equipment location
- Current use of equipment
- Current condition of equipment

And if the equipment has been disposed of, include:

- Final disposition of equipment and any corresponding sales price

 **Key Concepts**

- Property purchased with federal funds has compliance standards regardless of whether the property is federally owned or recipient-owned.

- Recipient must track and maintain complete and accurate records for property purchased with federal funds.

Chapter 3

Care and Use of Property

*A*ren't we taught as children that sharing is good? And don't we all want to be trusting people? When it comes to safeguarding property purchased with federal funds, sharing is not good and being less trusting is a requirement.

So maybe you think that one federal grant looks like another when it comes to property use. Or you think it's no big deal to put that property to use for the greater good of mankind. Start thinking "Stranger Danger!" As a federal grant recipient, you have responsibilities for keeping property safe from both external and internal threats.

Care and Use of Requirements

The care and use of property warrants a discussion in four key areas:

- The concept of controlled use
- The insurance requirements
- Specific state requirements
- The maintenance requirements
- The trust relationship between the recipient and the federal government as it relates to federally funded property

Controlled Use

Property purchased with federal funds may not be used for activities unrelated to the project or program objectives without approval of the awarding agency. The recipient has a duty to the federal government to restrict the use of property to only authorized activities.

Insurance

The recipient is required to provide equivalent insurance coverage for federally funded property titled in its own name as it does for non-federally funded property titled in its own name. When the recipient maintains federally funded property titled to the federal government, there is no requirement for insurance unless it is specifically required by the federal award terms and conditions. The federal government chooses to self-insure, that is, to pay for losses itself, when it has determined that doing so is preferable to having the recipient purchase insurance.

State Requirements

The grant guidance allows states to follow their own state laws and procedures for the use, management, and disposition of equipment that is acquired under a federal grant.

Maintenance

Recipients must have procedures in place to ensure that equipment purchased with federal funds is maintained, to keep the equipment in good condition.

Trust Relationship

Property purchased with federal funds must be held in trust for the beneficiaries of the federal program or project. The recipient steps in the shoes of the federal government to ensure the property is used as authorized by the awarding agency.

Recipients must ensure that property is adequately protected from loss, damage, and theft. There are many ways to accomplish this, from secure access to storage areas to proper training of employees who use equipment in the field. The best time to address adequate safeguards is prior to a loss. If equipment is lost, stolen, or damaged, the recipient must fully investigate and document the results of that investigation. For example, if a piece of equipment is stolen, a copy of the police report and insurance claim should be included with the documentation. If the equipment is federally owned, prompt notification to the awarding agency is required. A copy of the e-mail or other form of notification to the federal awarding agency should be included with the supporting documentation.

Key Concepts

- Property must be used only for authorized purposes.

- Insurance may be required.

- Maintenance procedures must be implemented.

- Recipients must comply with numerous requirements for property record keeping, tracking, and reporting.

Chapter 4

 # Disposition of Property

*D*o you like those hoarder reality television shows? It can be hard to say goodbye to all the stuff purchased with federal funds. Perhaps you have finished up all your grant work, or other changes have been made that mean the property purchased with federal funds is no longer needed.

The first step in the disposal process is for the grantee to ask the awarding agency for disposition instructions. Now's your chance to turn the tables on your federal agency and bug them for a change! You may be amazed at how hard it is to get disposal instructions, and how long it takes to actually get a decision. To paraphrase my kids, "Have you decided yet? Have you decided yet?"

Methods of Property Disposal

Property disposal requirements are often buried in the award terms and conditions. The method of disposal can depend on the type of the property being disposed of. Here are the general rules for property disposal:

Real Property

When the real property is no longer needed for the purpose that it was originally authorized for, the grantee should ask the awarding agency for disposition instructions.

When the federal agency directs that the real property be sold, sales procedures shall be followed to ensure competition for the sale. These procedures should be followed to the extent practicable, and result in the highest possible return on the sale of the property.

The federal government offers three primary options for disposing of real property.

- **Option 1:** The recipient retains title to the real property after compensating the federal government.
- **Option 2:** The federal awarding agency directs the recipient to sell the property.
- **Option 3:** The federal awarding agency directs the recipient to transfer title to the property to the federal government or an eligible third party.

Options 1 and 2 involve the federal government receiving their percentage share of the current fair market value of the property. The percentage of federal ownership is based on the federal awarding agency's percentage of participation in the original purchase. Under Option 2, the federal awarding agency is entitled to their share of the sale proceeds after actual and reasonable costs of fixing up and selling the property are deducted. Disposition of property under Option 3 entitles the recipient to receive its percentage share of the current fair market value, based on its participation in the real property purchase and any improvements made to the real property thereafter.

In all the cases, the federal government either gets a percentage share of the value or the real property after paying the recipient its share of the value.

Equipment

When equipment is no longer needed for the original project or program, there is an order of priority that is usually followed for redeploying the equipment. The first priority is that the equipment be offered for use in other federally supported activities. The second priority is to use the equipment for non-federally supported activities. The awarding agency should provide instructions on where to send unneeded equipment. If the equipment has a current fair market value over $5,000 at the time the equipment is no longer needed by the program or project, the recipient may retain the equipment for use in a non-federal activity if the awarding agency is compensated for the current fair market value.

If the federal awarding agency either doesn't respond to the request for disposal instructions within 120 days or directs the recipient to sell, the equipment may be sold. The federal awarding agency must be reimbursed for its share of the sales proceeds. The recipient must ensure that sales procedures provide for competition in the sales process to the extent practicable and result in the highest possible return.

On the flip side, if the recipient or subrecipient doesn't implement the appropriate disposition actions, including requesting instructions for disposition, the federal agency can step in and direct the recipient or subrecipient to take specific actions.

The recipient may also sell or trade-in equipment and purchase replacement equipment. The proceeds from the sale or trade-in will be used to offset the cost of the replacement equipment.

Supplies and Other Expendables

For supplies and other expendables, the recipient may use any remaining inventory to support non-federal activities or may just sell the residual inventory. In either of these cases, the federal government should be compensated for its portion of the proceeds from the sale or the non-federal use of the supplies and other expendables.

Intangible Property

The federal awarding agency retains the right to a royalty-free, nonexclusive and irrevocable right to use and authorize others to use federally funded intellectual property developed during the award period. The recipient should be aware that license fees and royalties on intellectual property could be considered program income during the award period. The federal awarding agency can provide specifics for disposing of intellectual property.

Key Concepts

- The awarding agency controls the method for disposing of property acquired with federal funds.

- The federal government usually benefits from the sale or transfer of the property to the extent it participated in the purchase.

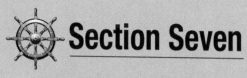 **Section Seven**

Procurement Standards

*D*o you feel like you are struggling to keep up with all the changes to the grant regulations in 2 CFR Part 200? Well hold on to your hat, because more changes to the procurement requirements have been released. The grace period for implementation of the new procurement standards contained in sections 2 CFR 200.317 through 200.326 has been extended to two fiscal years.

Now, this doesn't mean you don't have to comply with any procurement standards; it just means that you can choose to follow either the old or new regulations during this grace period. Additionally, the grant recipient is required to document its choice of which procurement standards it follows in the internal procurement policies.

Overview of Topics

In this section, we'll explore four main areas related to procurement standards:

- The requirements for written procedures in the procurement standards
- The elements that must be included in the written standards of conduct
- Various topics related to free and open competition in procurements
- Other contract issues, such as contract administration, contract requirements, and contract provisions

At the end of this section, you should recognize and understand the following:

- What elements and guidelines must be included in your written procurement procedures?
- Provisions that must be included in the written standards of conduct.
- Procurement practices that may inhibit free and open competition in procuring goods and services for federal awards.
- What documentation should be included with the procurement files?
- Which procurement procedures and guidelines must be in writing?

Chapter 1

Written Procedures

W*ritten procedure requirements must speak to the "necessity" of the purchase in order for the costs to be allowable for federal awards. So as a grant professional you may face this dilemma: Is this purchase really necessary for the efficient and effective management of the federal award? What do you think?*

In one organization many of the engineers stood in line at the Apple store to get the latest iPhone. Did they really need that for the effective management of the grant? In another grant office there was a heated discussion about the necessity of a Humvee for field work. Fortunately for that grant recipient and the reputation of that organization, the Ford F-150 won out.

Procurement Procedure Requirements

The procurement standards require two types of written procedures:

- Written procurement procedures covered in this chapter
- Written standard of conduct for the recipient covered in the next chapter

Non-federal entities can use their own documented procurement procedures, which must include the required applicable federal regulations and procurements standards. Procurement procedures must include guidelines that:

- Avoid unnecessary purchases
- Encourage partnering with state and local governments
- Promote use of federal excess and surplus property

- Promote use of value engineering clauses in construction contracts
- Require the use of responsible and reputable contractors
- Require recording the history of the procurement
- Discourage use of time and material type contracts
- Explain methods of procurement
- Solicit goods and services as required by the procurement standards

Avoid Unnecessary Purchases

The procurement standards require a written statement in the procurement procedure that says, "Recipients must avoid purchasing unnecessary items." From a practical standpoint, avoiding unnecessary purchases is not just the responsibility of the procurement department. Avoiding unnecessary purchases is a joint effort that involves the requisitioner, the purchase approver, and the purchasing department. This provision is targeted to avoid making purchases just because they are in the budget. The recipient is expected to purchase only items needed by the project or program to further the objectives of the award.

When the recipient has the option to either buy or lease goods, a lease vs. buy analysis must be performed. The analysis must determine which option is the most economical and practical. The recipient must document the results of the analysis. The analysis should be evaluated from the standpoint of the federal government. This may (or may not) be the most economical and practical option for the recipient.

Encourage Partnering With State and Local Governments

The OMB Super Circular procurement standards encourage partnering with state and local governments, when appropriate, for procurement or use of common or shared goods and services. Partnering in this manner promotes cost-efficiency.

Promote Use of Federal Excess and Surplus Property

Procurement guidelines encourage recipients to use federal excess or surplus property instead of purchasing new property, so as to reduce project costs.

Promote Use of Value Engineering Clauses in Construction Contracts

Value engineering analyzes each item in a contract to ensure that it's the best value at the lowest cost. The OMB Super Circular encourages the use of value engineering clauses in large construction contracts.

Require Use of Responsible and Reputable Contractors

The OMB Super Circular procurement procedures require the use of responsible and reputable contractors. Recipients must consider the integrity, past performance, competency, and other factors in the selection of contractors.

Require Recording the History of the Procurement

Procurements must be recorded in detail to satisfy the procurement procedures outlined in 2 CFR Part 200. Specifically, procurement records must show why a particular procurement method was chosen, the contract type, factors contributing to the selection and rejection of contractors, and the basis of the contract price.

Discourage Use of Time and Material-Type Contracts

Time and material-type contracts result in an open-ended contract price. This means that the contractor has no incentive to control costs or labor because the contract price has no ceiling. Under current OMB Super Circular procurement guidelines, recipients must only use time and material-type contracts when no other contract type is appropriate. When used, the recipient must enforce a ceiling on the contract price and tightly monitor the contract to ensure efficiency.

Procurement Methods

The methods for soliciting bids for goods and services should also be covered in the procurement procedures. 2 CFR Part 200 mandates five procurement methods for non-federal entities. The five methods are:

- Micro-purchase (not to exceed $3000-$2000 for Davis-Bacon Act)
- Small purchase (up to $150,000)
- Sealed bid
- Competitive proposal (greater than $150,000)
- Sole source proposal

Both the micro-purchase and small purchase methods include procedures for small purchases and generally contemplate a relatively simple and informal way to purchase goods and services. The micro-purchase does not require price quotes if the price is reasonable. In contrast the small purchase method, though still less formal, does require rate quotes from an adequate number of qualified sources.

The next method is the sealed-bid method, where bids are publicly solicited. This method usually involves formal advertising and results in a firm fixed-price contract being awarded to the lowest responsive and responsible bidder. In this method, the bids are publicly opened at a time and place designated in the invitation for bid. This method is usually preferred for construction contracts, and will involve at least two responsible bidders.

In contrast, the competitive proposal method may be used when conditions are not appropriate for sealed bids. This method is less formal than the sealed-bid method, but does involve publicizing and soliciting bids from an adequate number of qualified sources. The result is generally either a fixed price or cost-reimbursement contract.

Finally, the sole source proposal may be used when there are unique circumstances, such as a public emergency that do not allow for full and open competition. Generally, this type of procurement must be authorized by the federal agency or pass-through entity for subawardees.

Solicitation of Goods and Services

Solicitation of goods and services has several specific requirements in the written procurement procedures:

- The solicitation must include a description of the needed goods or services.
- This description must be clear, accurate, and spell out the technical requirements.
- The description should not contain elements that unduly restrict competition.

- The solicitation should describe what requirements the bidder is expected to fulfill.
- The solicitation should also include what factors will be used to evaluate the bids.
- The solicitation should describe the technical requirements for the procurement in terms of the functions to be performed.
- When the term "brand name or equivalent" is used in a solicitation, the specific features of that brand should be included.

The solicitation should include a range of acceptable characteristics or minimum standards. Avoid detailed product specifications. Remember, the overall goal of these standards is to not impair competition by needlessly restricting the technical specifications.

 **Key Concepts**

Written procurement procedures must include certain provisions that serve to lower and control project costs while ensuring value such as:

- Avoiding unnecessary purchases
- Ensuring full and open competition to the extent possible
- Soliciting goods and services as required by standards

Chapter 2

Chapter 2

Standards of Conduct

*J*n the past, conflicts of interest and standards of conduct were often treated as a game of hide-and-seek more than show-and-tell. Now, however, the overriding theme in grant guidance is increased responsibility for grantees. This means it's your responsibility to disclose any potential conflicts of interest to the federal awarding agency or pass-through entity.

No more waiting to see if the auditor finds them. No more waiting to see if the awarding agency or inspector general finds them. It's all on you as the grant recipient to be alert to potential conflicts of interest and let the Feds know if anything is amiss.

Standards of Conduct

The push for high levels of integrity and ethical behavior through the organization's standards of conduct is one of the ways that the federal government seeks to reduce the risk of waste, fraud and abuse of federal funds. The new grant regulations in 2 CFR Part 200 require non-federal entities to be alert to conflicts of interest and other violations, in addition to ramping up the disclosure requirements for grant recipients.

Who is Covered?

The written standard of conduct covers both employees working on federal awards and personnel involved in administering procurement contracts. The standard of conduct requirement specifically targets contracts supported by federal funds and covers employees, officers, and agents of the non-federal entity. The code of conduct requirements extends to include related parties of these individuals. A related party is defined to include members of the immediate family, partners, and even the related party's employer. The term "employer" could also include potential employers.

What Situations are Covered?

The written standard of conduct covers situations where either a real or apparent conflict of interest may be involved. The written standard of conduct requirement covers a wide list of relationships, not just a few key employees. An example of an apparent conflict of interest could be when the spouse of an employee is employed by a company bidding for work with the recipient. In this example, the non-federal entity must determine from the facts whether a real or apparent conflict of interest exists. If there is a conflict of interest, the individuals are prohibited from participating in the selection, award, or administration of the contract.

What is Prohibited?

The next part of the standard of conduct requirements states that employees, officers, and agents of the non-federal entity are expressly prohibited from soliciting or accepting gratuities, favors, or items of monetary value. This provision does allow the recipient to define at what level a gift is considered to be of nominal value or a non-substantial financial interest. For example, if a contractor offers a bottle of water during a meeting that would probably be considered of nominal value. If the contractor offered a flat-screen TV that would likely violate the written standard of conduct requirements.

Disciplinary Action

The written standard of conduct must include disciplinary actions for violations. Recipients must have a process in place to document that all covered parties are aware of the standard of conduct and the provisions contained within. The goal is to prevent violations, intentional or unintentional, from happening in the first place.

Key Concepts

- Recipients must have a written standard of conduct for individuals in the non-federal entity and for the non-federal entity that includes key elements covered in the procurement standards.

Chapter 3
Competition

airness is not just a term used by four-year-olds and politicians. The federal government is also in the mix, with requirements to spread the federal dollars around to businesses that may have been shut out of federal spending in the past.

And it's not enough to sit around waiting for under-served populations to come knocking on the door of your procurement office. You need to be finding ways to include them in your procurement process.

Competition Requirements

The four main areas related to competition discussed in the procurement standards include:

- Competitive and non-competitive practices, including conflicts of interest
- Cost-price analysis
- Affirmative steps to support women- and/or minority-owned businesses

Competitive Practices

The procurement standards require procurement transactions to support "free and open" competition to the "maximum extent practicable." Promoting competition in procurement transactions is at the core of this guidance. Please note that the term free and open competition is also referred to as full and open competition in some publications.

The procurement standards require awarding bids that are most advantageous to the recipient, as opposed to awarding bids on such non-competitive factors as personal preferences. The decision on awarding bids should be the best outcome after taking into account price, quality, and other relevant factors, such as delivery and warranty.

The procurement standards state the recipient has the right to reject all bids when it is in their best interest to do so. This means that the competition requirements do not extend to the point that the recipient must always accept the lowest bid, if it is not in the best interests of the non-federal entity to do so.

Avoid Non-Competitive Practices

In addition to avoiding non-competitive practices in their procurements, recipients must also be alert to non-competitive practices of outside contractors. This is another example of how the recipient steps in the shoes of the federal agency to monitor compliance in lower-tier non-federal entities.

Recipients must also be aware that the procurement standards expressly prohibit awarding work to a contractor that develops the specifications, requirements, statement of work, or other related documents that are used to solicit bids. The goal with this requirement is to prevent a contractor from unduly influencing the solicitation for goods or services.

Examples of non-competitive practices may include:

- Awarding work when there is either a real or apparent conflict of interest
- Soliciting work from a sole source without an acceptable written justification
- Awarding work to the contractor that developed the specifications used in the solicitation

The federal awarding agency may require the recipient to submit supporting documentation if certain conditions exist during the procurement process, such as:

- Procurement transactions made when the non-federal entity's procurement process didn't meet procurement standards contained in 2 CFR Part 200
- Procurements that require a brand name in the specifications
- An award made to someone other than the apparent low bidder

Conflict of Interest

The recipient is required to be alert to conflicts of interest in its procurement transactions. This means the recipient needs to establish a procedure for identifying and communicating potential conflicts of interest. Please refer to the part on the written standard of conduct requirements for additional conflict-of-interest topics.

Cost-Price Analysis

For every procurement action in excess of the Simplified Acquisition Threshold (currently at $150,000) 2 CFR Part 200 requires some form of cost or price analysis. A price analysis ensures that the price paid by the federal award is competitive within the market place. Therefore, the price analysis needs to demonstrate the non-federal entity's efforts at ensuring free and open competition. There are many different ways to document this effort, including comparison of price quotes and reviewing examples of market prices. The cost analysis reviews all associated costs to make sure the costs are reasonable, allocable, and allowable by the federal award.

The cost-price analysis should be included with the procurement documentation. The extent of the cost-price analysis is determined by the amount of procurement. This analysis could range from minimal analysis for a micro-purchase to greater analysis for a procurement that falls under the Simplified Acquisition Threshold and uses small-purchase methods.

The greater the amount spent, the greater the responsibility for ensuring a competitive price. Ultimately, a combination of federal regulations and internal organizational policies determines the amount of documentation required to support the cost-price analysis. If you have specific questions for your non-federal entity, please talk with your contracting officer.

Affirmative Steps

The OMB Super Circular procurement standards require that recipients take "affirmative steps" to use minority businesses, women-owned businesses, and small businesses when possible.

Affirmative steps must include:

- Placing qualified small, minority-owned, and women-owned businesses on solicitation lists
- Making information about upcoming procurements available to small, minority-owned, and women-owned businesses whenever they are potential sources
- Dividing total requirements into smaller tasks or quantities to allow for participation by small, minority-owned, and women-owned businesses. If a single procurement is expected to be too large for any one small business, the recipient should encourage the use of consortiums of small businesses to facilitate participation.

- Planning the time frame for procurements to actively encourage and facilitate patronizing small, minority-owned, and women-owned businesses
- Using the services of organizations such as the Small Business Administration during the solicitation process
- Requiring subcontractors to take the same affirmative steps

Taking affirmative steps to use minority businesses, women-owned business, and small businesses is a mandatory procurement requirement in 2 CFR Part 200.

 **Key Concepts**

- The goal in the procurement standards is to enable free and open competition to the extent practicable.

- The recipient must be aware of practices that inhibit competition. This responsibility extends not just to the recipient, but also to subrecipients and subcontractors.

- Active inclusion of small businesses and minority- and women-owned firms is not just nice to do, but is a federal mandate.

- Affirmative steps are a requirement for receiving federal funds.

Chapter 4

Contracts

. . . .

*D*oesn't it seem like the list of documentation requirements for federal grants is endless? Procurement is an area of grant management that requires lots of record keeping and documentation Yes, it does seem like even more documentation is needed than in other areas of grant management!

When it comes to spending federal funds, there may be many different people requesting things, but the purchasing department is where the auditors focus their laser beam. That's because procurement is viewed as one of the first lines of defense against improper spending of grant funds.

Contract Topics

Three main areas related to contracts merit detailed discussion:

- Contract administration
- Contract requirements
- Certain contract provisions

Contract Administration

The recipient must have contract administration systems in place to ensure that contractors are conforming to the terms, conditions, and specifications of the contract. The recipient must also have a process to follow up on purchases to determine if the purchases are received in a timely and complete manner. Contract administration involves the process of evaluating contractors and the related documentation of the results of that evaluation.

The documentation for contractors should look at such topics as whether the contractor met the contract terms, conditions, and specifications.

The recipient should include the following items in the procurement files for any purchases in excess of the Simplified Acquisition Threshold:

- The basis for the contractor selection
- The basis for the price or cost of the purchase
- A written justification, if applicable, documenting the reasons for the lack of competition on the procurement; for example, on a sole-source purchase

Contract Requirements

The procurement standards generally let the recipient determine the type of contract, or procuring instrument. However, the contract type must be appropriate for promoting the best interests of the project or program. The procurement standards specifically prohibit the use of cost-plus-percentage-of-cost or percentage-of-construction-cost contracts.

Most contracts are either fixed-price or cost-reimbursement contracts. A fixed-price contract is used when there are complete product descriptions or specifications. The result is a fixed price to provide the products or services.
A cost-reimbursement contract may be used when it is not feasible or appropriate to award a fixed-price contract. For example, a cost-reimbursement contract may be appropriate if the work involves significant technical unknowns, such as engineering or consulting services.

There are a few other variations in the contract requirements that we will examine. Let's look at differences between cost-type contracts and percentage–of-completion contracts.

The cost-type contract is used when the contractor is paid based on the actual costs the contractor has incurred. In a percentage–of-completion contract, payments are made for construction work based on the percentage of work completed instead of the actual costs incurred. Grantees may use percentage–of-completion contracts, but should be aware that federal agencies reimburse only for the actual costs incurred on this type of contract.

The procurement standard specifically prohibits the use of cost-plus–a-percentage-of-cost or percentage-of-construction-cost contracts. This prohibition is because this type of cost-plus contract can be an incentive for contractors to increase the project costs to increase their profit.

The procurement standard also requires that contracts be made with contractors who possess the ability to perform successfully on the contract. The recipient may consider such factors as contractor integrity, past performance, and technical and financial resources when evaluating this contract requirement.

Contract Provisions

When a grant recipient issues a contract to a contractor there are numerous contract provisions listed in the grant regulations that potentially must be included. Some of these contract provisions may be required regardless of the size of the procurement. Please refer to Section Two for a more extensive list of the various contract provisions contained in 2 CFR Part 200.

In addition to the contract provisions, the procurement standard requires that all contracts in excess of the Simplified Acquisition Threshold (currently set at $150,000) include contract provisions for termination of the contract by the recipient. There must also be contract provisions to terminate the contract for circumstances beyond the contractor's control and a provision for remedies if the contractor violates the terms of the contract.

The procurement standard goes on to add requirements for contract provisions allowing the recipient or the federal government to inspect documents of the contractor that are directly related to the program or project. This contract provision is required on negotiated contracts in excess of the Simplified Acquisition Threshold.

 **Key Concepts**

- Procurements in excess of the Simplified Acquisition Threshold must document certain items in the procurement files, including: the basis for selecting the contractor, the basis for the price, and an evaluation of the contractor's performance.

Section Eight

Closeout of Federal Awards

It's a Cinderella moment. You know the one. The clock strikes midnight and the beautiful carriage turns into a pumpkin. Grant spending is like that. Once the period of performance is over, the party's over. Avoid having your grant fairy tale turn into a nightmare by understanding the real-life closeout requirements.

Overview of Topics

In this section, we'll see four main areas related to general roles and responsibilities for federal award recipients:

- An overview of the closeout process
- The requirements for record retention
- Termination and enforcement of awards
- Procedures and related topics for closing out an award
- The conditions for subsequent adjustments after the award has closed

At the end of this section, you should recognize and understand the following:

- The main steps in the award close-out process
- Requirements for record retention
- How an award may be terminated and the remedies for enforcement of award terms and conditions
- Main issues related to closing out an award
- When subsequent adjustments may be made after an award has closed

Chapter 1

Overview of the Closeout Process

*S*how me the money! As you start the closeout process, either
your organization or the funding agency will be shouting this
out. Show me the money! It's time to settle up.

Closeout Process

After an award expires, the closeout process begins. During
this process, the federal awarding agency determines if all
applicable administrative actions and all associated work
have been completed by the federal award recipient.
All allowable costs should be promptly reimbursed by the
federal awarding agency. Generally, the final drawdown of
federal funds should be completed no later than ninety days
after the award end date and submission of a final financial
status report.

A final review of the award is required to ensure all closeout
requirements are met.

The following transactions and their related reports as
indicated by the terms and conditions of the award are
required during the closeout process:

• A refund of any unobligated cash balances not
  authorized by the federal awarding agency for retention by
  the federal award recipient

- A settlement of any upward or downward adjustments to the federal share of costs, if any

- An accounting of any real or personal property acquired with federal funds during the award period

The federal awarding agency may request additional supporting documents, such as:

- Records of completed training
- Resolution of any outstanding compliance issues
- Program records demonstrating full implementation of the award objectives

It is important to note that violations of award requirements may result in:

- Ineligibility for future funding
- Requests for reimbursement of misused award funds
- Other measures which the federal agencies may take to remedy the award violations

 **Key Concepts**

- Grant closeout is a process of settling all obligations and reconciling the actual award expenditures with reimbursements or award advances.

- In most cases, the final drawdown of federal funds should be completed no later than ninety days after the award end date and submission of a final financial status report.

Chapter 2
Record Retention

*A*re you facing the Goldilocks Dilemma of record retention? Is your record retention too much? Not enough? Or just right? Wondering which records to keep for your federal grant record-retention requirements and which ones can be tossed? This is an area that gets many federal grant recipients into trouble.

Types of Records

The record-retention process during closeout includes a variety of record types including:

- Financial records
- Procurement records
- Cost-sharing documentation
- Real property and equipment records
- Indirect cost rate proposals
- Other types of records such as suspension and debarment compliance documentation

Record-retention requirements also exist for indiret cost rate proposals and cost-allocation plans. The federal recipient must retain all other records that may be pertinent to the award, such as program documentation and other compliance records.

Financial Records

Financial records should include the source documentation that supports the financial and accounting records. Some examples of these records include:

- Copies of paid bills
- Cancelled checks and bank statements
- Support for payroll and time and attendance records
- Copies of contracts and subgrant or subaward documents
- Copies of prior-authorization approval documents, as required

Procurement Records

Next, the procurement history files should contain supporting records such as:

- The procurement method rationale
- Backup for the contract type selection and basis for the contractor selection or rejection
- The basis for the contract price, which would generally include a price or cost analysis
- Evidence of prior approval for those items that required prior approval on the procurement

Cost Sharing Documentation

When it comes to cost-sharing or matching records, the federal recipient is required to maintain documentation that supports the determination of the cost-share valuation. This could include formal appraisals when required or other supporting records such as a comparison of market values for donated labor or property.

Real Property and Equipment Records

Moving on to real property and equipment records, the federal recipient should be aware that there are extensive record-keeping requirements. Property records should contain the following data:

- A description of the property that contains a unique identifier such as a serial number
- The cost and source of the property; for example, the contractor name if purchased
- Whether title is held by the federal government or the federal recipient
- The date the property was acquired and the percentage of federal participation in the acquisition cost

The federal recipient may also have continuing documentation requirements for real property and equipment, such as tracking the following items:

- The current location of the property
- The current use and condition

If the property is not in use, also include:

- The disposition instructions
- The date of disposal
- The sales price received from the disposal, if applicable

Indirect Cost Rate Proposals

Moving on to indirect cost records, the retention requirements include all rate proposals without regard to whether they were submitted for negotiation.

The supporting documentation could contain:

- Indirect cost rate proposals
- Cost-allocation plans
- Accounting computations
- Other documents that support the rate computations, such as computer usage charge-back rates and the composition of fringe-benefit or facility rates

Other Records

Finally, the federal recipient is required to retain other records that are pertinent to the federal award, such as:

- Evidence of subrecipient monitoring
- Evidence of suspension and debarment compliance, such as screen shots of an excluded-parties list system search
- Program records that support program accomplishments and reporting
- Evidence of contract provisions compliance for the federal recipient and (if applicable) the subrecipients and contractors. An example of contract provisions compliance is documentation for Davis-Bacon Act requirements.

Please note that these sample record types are not meant to be an all-inclusive list of what records the federal recipient must retain, but are a selection of the major categories.

Time Frame

The general rule for record retention is that records must be retained for three years from the date of submission of the final expenditure report. If the federal awarding agency authorizes and the federal recipient submits quarterly or annual reports, the three-year time frame will start from the date of submission of the annual or quarterly expenditure report.

The three-year record retention rule has some exceptions:

Property Records

Real property and equipment records must be retained for three years from the date of final disposition of the property.

Depending on the use of the property, this could be considerably longer than three years from the date of award completion.

Litigation and Other Claims

Litigation cases, claims or audits started before the three-year period expires extend the retention period. In these cases, the federal award recipient must retain records until all actions have been resolved and final action related to the litigation, claims, or audits has been taken.

Indirect Cost Allocation

For indirect cost rate proposals, allocation plans, and other related records the three year retention period starts on a different date than the general rule. In the case of plans submitted for negotiation, the records must be retained for three years from the date of submission. If the indirect cost rate proposal or allocation plan was not submitted for negotiation, the records must be retained for three years from the end of the covered fiscal year.

Request for Extended Retention

The federal awarding agency or other agency that approves the indirect cost rates (called the cognizant agency) can submit a written request to the federal award recipient to extend the three-year retention period.

Discoverable Records

When the federal awarding agency or pass-through entity chooses to maintain the records they become "discoverable" and available for record requests. In this case the three-year retention period does not apply to the federal award recipient.

Program Income

When program income is earned after end of performance period, the terms and conditions of the grant may require reporting of program income earned after the performance period ends. In this case, the retention period for these records begins at the end of the federal award recipient's fiscal year during which the program income was earned.

Right of Access

The federal government and its duly authorized representatives have a right to access federal recipient records in a timely and reasonable manner. The records must be pertinent to the award in question. This right to access by the federal government includes:

- The right to timely and reasonable access to the federal award recipient's personnel
- The right to interview and discuss documents that are pertinent to the award with the Federal recipient's personnel

Note that the federal government's right to access records extends as long as records are retained and without limit to the three-year retention period requirements. For example, if a company does not dispose of records after the three-year retention requirements have expired, the federal funding agency can request all records related to the federal award, regardless of the age of the records.

Public Access

Federal awarding agencies are prohibited from placing restrictions on federal award recipients that limit public access to records related to federal awards, except in the following circumstances:

- The federal agency can demonstrate that the records should be kept confidential and that they would have been exempt from Freedom of Information Act (FOIA) disclosures or executive orders related to controlled unclassified information.

- To protect Personally Identifiable Information (PII). Protected PII includes a person's first name or first initial and last name combined with one or more types of information including, but not limited to, social security number, passport number, credit card numbers, clearances, bank numbers, biometrics, date and place of birth, mother's maiden name, and criminal, medical, and financial records, educational transcripts. This exception does not include PII required by law to be disclosed.

Federal award recipients are not required to allow public access to their records unless required to do so by federal, state, or local statutes.

 **Key Concepts**

- Federal recipient records related to federal awards must be maintained for three years following the final report to the federal funding agency, with some exceptions.

- The federal government retains the right to timely and unrestricted access to pertinent federal recipient records and personnel.

Chapter 3

Termination and Enforcement of Awards

*H*earing the word termination can bring to mind many different things. Sometimes in the termination of a relationship, it is a friendly divorce. Other times, not so much...

Termination

The word "termination" for the purpose of this regulation means the withdrawal of authority to obligate funds before that authority would have otherwise expired. In other words, the federal recipient loses the right to spend money before the end of the award period.

The federal awarding agency may terminate an award in whole or in part when the following conditions exist:

- The federal recipient materially fails to comply with the terms and conditions of the federal award
- The federal awarding agency has cause to terminate
- The federal recipient and the federal awarding agency mutually agree to terminate the award

In cases when the federal recipient and the federal agency mutually agree to terminate the award in whole or in part, the federal recipient must take the following steps:

- The federal recipient needs to send the federal awarding agency written notification of termination, including the reasons for the termination and the effective date of termination.

When the federal awarding agency terminates a federal award, it must send the federal award recipient a notice of termination. The notice will state, among other things, that the termination decision may be considered in future applications.

Enforcement

The federal government has many methods for enforcing the terms and conditions of federal awards, including:

- The right to temporarily withhold cash payments from the federal recipient
- The right to disallow all or part of a project's costs
- The right to wholly or partially suspend the award
- The right to withhold further awards from the federal recipient
- Take other legally available remedies

When an enforcement action is contemplated by a federal agency, the federal awarding agency must provide opportunities to the federal recipient for hearings, appeals, and other administrative proceedings.

 **Key Concepts**

- The federal government has the right to terminate an award in whole or part if the federal recipient is not in compliance with the terms and conditions of the award, or for cause.
- The federal recipient and the agency may mutually agree to terminate an award in whole or part.
- The federal agency can withhold payments to the federal recipient or disallow costs to force compliance with the terms and conditions of the award.

Chapter 4

Closeout Procedures

*I*t's said that all good things must come to an end. Closeout is the process that consists of many actions, including final reporting for the award, disposition of property, and record-retention requirements. The awarding agency may have additional requirements, such as reports about the accomplishment of program objectives and other key metrics.

Three Areas of Closeout

The chapter discusses three main areas related to closeout procedures:

- Closeout reports
- Settlement of federal recipient obligations and payments
- Ongoing responsibilities the federal recipient has to the federal government, even after the award is closed

Closeout is defined as the process a federal awarding agency goes through to determine if all applicable administrative actions have been completed. The federal awarding agency will also check that all work required by the terms and conditions of the award have been completed.

The term "date of completion" is defined as the date on which all work under an award is completed or the date stated on the award document as when federal sponsorship ends. The award documents include any supplements or amendments that contain a date of completion.

Reporting

Several actions precede the closeout of a federal award by a federal awarding agency. First, the federal awarding agency must receive all required reports from the federal recipient. Next, the federal awarding agency must make prompt payments to the federal award recipient for any allowable reimbursable costs. The federal awarding agency must also determine the disposition or recovery of any federally owned property. Finally, a final adjustment of the award amount and the amount of cash paid to the federal recipient will be made to reconcile expenditures against the amount of federal funds drawn by the federal recipient.

Before the end of the award period, the federal awarding agency must notify the federal recipient, in writing, of the due date for the final reports and provide a list of the required forms, with instructions. Generally, unless the federal awarding agency approves an extension, all financial, performance, and other required reports are due within ninety calendar days of award completion. The federal awarding agency then has one year to complete closeout of the federal award.

Settlement

Similar to the reporting requirements, unless the federal awarding agency approves an extension, the federal recipient is required to liquidate all outstanding obligations within ninety calendar days of award completion.

This means that the federal recipient has ninety days to settle all existing obligations to vendors and subcontractors following the completion of the award.

These regulations also require that the federal awarding agency make prompt payments to the federal recipient for any remaining allowable costs outstanding. Last, a final adjustment of the award amount and the amount of cash paid to the federal recipient will be made to reconcile expenditures against the amount of federal funds drawn by the federal recipient. The federal recipient must also return to the federal awarding agency any unobligated cash that was drawn.

Ongoing Responsibilities

A federal recipient has ongoing responsibilities in three main areas at the end of a federal award:

- Accounting and reporting on real and personal property purchased with federal funds as required by the federal awarding agency and other Federal regulations
- Accounting and reporting of program income earned post-award period, if applicable.
- Retaining records related to the federal award as required by the federal awarding agency and other federal regulations

Note when it comes to retaining records, there are a couple of notable exceptions to the three year record retention rule discussed in Chapter Two. The first has to do with ongoing responsibilities for property records retention that starts from the date the property is disposed of, replaced, or transferred. The second area concerns the responsibility to retain program income records beginning at the end of the federal award recipient's fiscal year during which the income was earned. So, the three-year timeframe doesn't begin at end of the award period, when it comes to property and program income.

Key Concepts

- Unless the federal awarding agency extends the time frame, the federal recipient must submit all required reports to the federal awarding agency and settle any outstanding obligation within ninety days.

- The federal recipient has ongoing responsibilities to the federal awarding agency to retain all relevant records and comply with property reporting requirements. These ongoing requirements can extend far beyond the end of the award period.

Chapter 5

 # Subsequent Adjustments

*J*o quote Yogi Berra, "It's like déjà vu all over again." Sometimes after you think you are done with your grant, things pop up. It could be a refund from a vendor. It could be a change in your indirect costs, or an audit adjustment made months after you submit the final report. Wondering what to do?

Subsequent Adjustments to Closed Awards

The regulations do provide for subsequent adjustments to a closed award. Subsequent adjustments can be made by the federal awarding agency, based on audits or other reviews. The agency may disallow costs based on this review and request the return of funds from the federal recipient. The federal recipient has a responsibility to return funds to the federal awarding agency resulting from refunds, corrections, and other types of transactions after the close of the federal award.

Finally, the federal awarding agency can make upward or downward adjustments to the federal share of costs, such as indirect costs, after the closeout reports have been received. The authority for these types of subsequent adjustments should appear in the terms and conditions of the federal award.

 **Key Concepts**

- Subsequent adjustments are allowed to closed awards, based on later audits or other types of reviews.

- Subsequent adjustments are also allowed if the federal recipient receives refunds or makes other types of corrections after closing the award.

- Federal regulations provide for subsequent adjustments based on changes in the federal share of costs, such as a change in the final indirect cost allocation rates.

Section Nine
Cost Principles for Direct Costs

irect costs are the where the majority of federal funding occurs. This category represents the people, products, and services supporting the implementation of the project objectives. And similarly, this is where the federal agencies want to spend the bulk of their time monitoring projects and programs. Unfortunately, this is where the least training occurs on how to manage a grant correctly. My mission is to change that short-sighted view of grant management and get the information into the hands of those who spend most of the federal dollars.

Overview of Topics

In this section, we'll look at four main areas related to direct costs:

- Basic requirements of award costs
- Various other direct cost topics, such as consistency of cost treatment
- The components of cost included in the direct cost base used for calculating the indirect cost rates
- Examples of direct costs

At the end of this section, you should recognize and understand the following:

- Requirements for allowable award costs
- Criteria for classifying costs as either direct or indirect costs
- Main types of costs included in the direct cost base
- Examples of direct costs that may be incurred by your organization

Chapter 1

🧩 Basics of Cost

*J*o quote Will Rogers, *"You can't legislate…common sense into people."* Yet this is exactly what the Cost Principles are trying to do with setting a hurdle of reasonableness on the allowability of costs for federal awards. They even have a name for it, and it's called the *"prudent person"* standard.

Cost Basics

This chapter covers these four key topics related to basics of cost:

- The composition of award costs
- Allowable costs
- Reasonable costs
- Allocable costs

Composition of Award Cost

We will begin with the main objectives of federal cost principles and standards as outlined in 2 CFR Part 200. The first objective is to provide a uniform approach for determining the costs that can be charged to federal awards. The next objective is to provide a mechanism for federal awards to bear their fair share of costs recognized under the regulations. Finally, federal cost principles should promote effective and efficient program delivery by setting standards and principles for program management.

The application of the Cost Principles is based on the following fundamental premises:

The first premise is that the non-federal entity is responsible for the efficient and effective administration of the federal award through the application of sound management practices.

Second, the non-federal entity shall use the federal funds in a manner that is consistent with the program objectives and the terms and conditions of the federal award.

Third, the federal government recognizes that every non-federal entity brings its own unique combination of staff, facilities, and experience to employ sound organization and management techniques necessary for achieving the proper and efficient administration of federal awards.

According to 2 CFR Part 200, total award costs are one of two types:

- Allowable direct costs
- Allowable indirect costs

Unallowable direct costs and unallowable indirect costs are not included in award costs. However, the award recipient may still be required to track unallowable costs in both direct and indirect cost categories.

Award costs include "applicable credits." Applicable credits are simply items that reduce the expenses of an award, such as purchase discounts, rebates, refunds, and insurance recoveries. The concept here is that the credits should follow the costs. For example, if a laptop is purchased for an award, any rebate received should be credited to the same purchase account as the laptop and not put into a different non-award rebate or expense account.

This is a great place for us refresh your understanding of some of this terminology. Specifically:

- Direct costs
- Indirect costs

Direct costs are costs that can be attributed to a particular final cost objective, such as a federally funded project or program. Direct costs can also be attributed to non-federally funded activities. The point is that direct costs are incurred for an identifiable final cost objective.

On the other hand, *indirect costs* are incurred for joint or common objectives that generally can't be easily identified with a particular final cost objective, such as a project or program. Indirect costs are frequently thought of as costs for support or administrative services. Examples of indirect costs include costs for accounting, human resources, and purchasing departments.

Allowable Costs

As we covered in the section on written procedures, each federal award recipient must have policies in place to assure that only allowable costs are charged to the federal award. Let's explore what makes costs allowable.

Award costs include only allowable direct and indirect costs. According to 2 CFR Part 200, allowability of costs applies to both direct and indirect costs. For costs to be allowable, they must first pass the hurdle of being reasonable and allocable. Next, costs must not be limited or excluded by 2 CFR Part 200. The federal award recipient must demonstrate that it applies policies uniformly to all activities, not just federal awards. Finally, allowable costs must be adequately documented.

Reasonable Costs

According to 2 CFR Part 200, the reasonable cost standard means that the amount of expenditure doesn't exceed the amount a prudent person would spend under the circumstances and at the time the decision was made to purchase the item. This is sometimes called the "prudent person standard."

Think of it this way: for costs to be considered reasonable for federal awards, the federal recipient must act with good sense in considering its responsibility to the federal government, the public (specifically the taxpayers), and where applicable, its students, membership, or other stakeholders. This means that federal recipient must consider the best interests of the various parties involved.

One way to look at reasonable costs would be to ask the following questions:

- Can I reasonably expect to use the amount of the product or services I am purchasing?
- Did I pay a fair price for the item(s)?
- Am I comfortable defending this purchase to a taxpayer or the federal agency?

Reasonableness also looks at the necessity of the purchase. For example would the costs generally be recognized as ordinary and necessary for the operation of the organization or for award performance? Let's dig into this a little deeper:

Necessary costs are defined as costs that are needed for the performance or administration of the federal award. Questions that test the necessity of a purchase include:

- Do I really need to make this purchase for the award?
- Is this the least amount I can spend and still meet my needs for the efficient and effective performance of the award?

Other considerations used in determining reasonableness of costs include determining if the cost is consistent with generally accepted sound business practices and arm's-length bargaining. The federal agency may look at the market prices for comparable goods and services in assessing whether the costs are reasonable.

Next, the costs may be viewed to see if the costs were incurred with significant deviations from established practices. Actions that unjustifiably increase the costs to the federal government would not be considered reasonable, according to the regulations. Remember, if costs are not defendable as reasonable, they risk being disallowed by the federal awarding agency.

Allocable Costs

Allocable costs are costs that can be allocated in accordance with the relative benefit received by that activity. Allocable costs are costs that are treated consistently with other costs incurred for the same purpose in like circumstances. Let's call this the fairness standard. Costs must be treated consistently with other costs incurred for the same purpose in like circumstances.

The federal government doesn't want to pay an unfair portion of costs compared to others participating in the same activity in like circumstances.

For example, a recipient could not charge a federal award a higher labor rate, and charge a non-federal award a lower labor rate for the same person performing the same activity in like circumstances.

Note that 2 CFR Part 200 also explicitly states that non-federal award recipients can't allocate costs between federal awards just to get around funding deficiencies or to avoid restrictions placed by the terms and conditions of the award or other federal regulations.

 **Key Concepts**

- Award costs consist of both allowable direct costs and allowable indirect costs.
- For costs to be considered allowable, they must be both reasonable and allocable.
- Costs must not be limited by 2 CFR Part 200 Cost Principles.
- Costs must be treated consistently within the organization.
- All costs must be adequately documented.

Chapter 2

Other
Direct Cost Topics

* *

*T*he new grant regulations rewrite parts of the guidance to
eliminate several areas of concern to grant recipients, including
clarifying the circumstances when administrative costs can be
included in direct costs. Hint: this is a huge opportunity for grant
recipients to budget for legitimate positions supporting programs
that in the past may have been grouped with indirect costs.
However, you must plan ahead and include these in your award
proposal and budget.

*Also, the ongoing argument about whether computers are
equipment or supplies has been settled. The OMB has ruled that
computing devices that fall under the capitalization level for
equipment can be treated as supplies and not be subject to the
onerous equipment tracking and reporting requirements.*

Direct Cost Topics

We will now cover a number of other direct cost topics. To
start, we will consider the requirement for costs to be treated
consistently in determining whether they are direct or indirect
costs. Next, we will look at the allowance for cost treatment of
minor cost amounts. Finally, we will examine the prohibition
on mixing or commingling direct costs from various final cost
objectives.

Note that the concept of consistency of cost treatment is one
of the main underpinnings of federal cost principles.

Consistency of Cost Treatment

The OMB Super Circular states that if a federal award recipient classifies costs as indirect costs, then the recipient may not also classify costs incurred for the same purpose in like circumstances as direct costs. The goal here is to not have a non-federal award recipient artificially moving costs between direct and indirect cost categories. For example, if you have two employees working in like circumstances for identical purposes, you are prohibited from classifying one of the employees as direct labor and one as indirect labor. This principle was widely interpreted to mean that administrative or support staff could not be charged directly to the federal award. Fortunately 2 CFR Part 200.413 clarifies the specific conditions that make direct charging of administrative or support staff to a federal award possible without violating the consistency of cost treatment principle.

Minor Amounts

The regulations provide for federal award recipients to treat minor amounts of direct costs as indirect costs for reasons of practicality, as long as this cost treatment is consistently applied to all types of awards. Again, the goal is consistency of cost treatment, and not unfairly moving costs between cost categories.

Commingling of Costs

This may seem obvious, but direct costs of an award can't include direct costs that meet the final cost objective for a different award. When a recipient has multiple awards, it is important for employees to understand that direct costs must be separated into the specific cost objective. Direct costs are not just all one big bucket of federal funds. The federal award recipient must segregate all the direct costs into the correct award direct cost buckets. Finally, the recipient may not include cost-sharing funds in direct costs.

Key Concepts

- One of the overarching goals of federal cost principles is to prevent artificial classification of costs as direct or indirect costs.

- If costs are incurred for the same purpose under like circumstances, then they must be treated consistently as either indirect costs or direct costs.

- Direct costs must follow the final cost objectives of the specific award for which the costs were incurred.

Chapter 3
Direct Cost Base

*W*ithout going all "math" on you, I want to emphasize the importance of understanding the implications that increasing the size of your base, i.e. the bottom part of the fraction used in calculating your indirect cost rate, can make in the new environment of 2 CFR Part 200. When you have a larger base to spread your indirect costs against, the indirect cost rate goes down. This is a trend that the Federal government wants to support in the coming years.

Composition of the Direct Cost Base

This chapter covers these four key topics related to direct cost base:

- Appropriate times to include both allowable and unallowable direct costs in the direct cost base
- Types of items included in Modified Total Direct Costs
- Types of costs excluded from the Modified Total Direct Costs

This is a great place for us to look at the terminology, specifically:

- Direct cost base
- Modified Total Direct Costs

Direct Cost Base

The "direct cost base" is generally the sum of all allowable direct costs from all awards, and certain unallowable direct costs. Direct costs that may be unallowable for the purpose of federal awards may be included in the direct cost base if the activities include costs for personnel and facilities that are supported by indirect cost activities, such as fund raising.

Modified Total Direct Costs

"Modified Total Direct Costs" (MTDC) includes the direct cost base reduced by certain exclusions. The goal of using MTDC rather than the direct cost base is to allocate indirect costs across a cost base that best measures the degree of benefits received. The modifications are used to remove items that may distort the share of indirect costs allocated to an award.

Allowable vs. Unallowable Costs in the Distribution Base

Unallowable direct costs for federal awards may need to be included in the direct cost base for the purpose of allocating indirect costs when the following conditions apply:

- The costs must be identified with a particular final cost objective to be considered direct costs.
- The direct costs must involve activities that include personnel and facilities and receive benefits or support from the federal award recipient's indirect costs.

Some examples of unallowable direct costs that should be included in the direct cost base include:

- Support and maintenance of the federal award recipient's membership
- Promotion, lobbying, and public relations activities
- Providing non-award-related services and information to the federal award recipient's members or to the public
- Fund-raising costs

The distribution base includes total direct costs reduced by certain exclusions. The goal of using a modified distribution base rather than total direct costs as the base is to allocate indirect costs across a cost base that best measures the degree of benefits received. The modifications are used to remove items that may distort the share of indirect costs allocated to an award.

Calculating Modified Total Direct Cost (MTDC)

MTDC starts with the total direct cost base and then excludes specific type of costs. The types of direct costs included in modified total direct costs can be as broad as the types of direct costs supporting the federally sponsored activities.

MTDC Components

MTDC generally includes:

- Direct salaries and related fringe benefits
- Direct materials and supplies
- Direct travel costs

MTDC Purpose

Modified total direct costs are used as the base to calculate the indirect cost rates. Indirect cost rates are calculated by dividing the total allowable indirect costs by the modified total direct cost base. For example, if your total indirect costs are $1 million and your modified total direct costs are $10 million, you would have an indirect cost-rate percentage of ten percent.

MTDC Exclusions

The following items are generally excluded from the MTDC:

- Capital expenditures
- Equipment purchases
- Costs of participant support, if applicable to your award
- The portion of any subawards in excess of $25,000

The limit to the first $25,000 of a subaward applies regardless of the period covered by the subaward. Finally, the federal award recipient's cognizant agency can exclude other items if they feel the items may distort the indirect cost allocation.

 **Key Concepts**

- The direct cost base may include both allowable and unallowable direct costs.

- The Modified Total Direct Cost base is used in computing the indirect cost rate that will be applied to direct costs of an award.

- The Modified Total Direct Cost base is used instead of the direct cost base for calculating the indirect cost rate to minimize distorting the amount of indirect costs applied when compared with the indirect cost benefits received.

Chapter 4

Examples of Direct Costs

*ack in 1980, I worked at a U.S. Census Bureau field office,
processing payroll. It may sound funny to say this today, but
picture this: all of our office furnishings (with the exception of our
chairs) were made out of cardboard. The desks, the file cabinets —
everything was wood-grain printed cardboard. Evidently someone
had done a study and decided it was more cost-effective to furnish
each field office with cardboard furniture that could be thrown
into the Dumpster at the end of the census, than to buy or rent
regular office furniture. The disposable furniture (and as temporary
workers, disposable people) had a negative impact on the morale and
engagement of the whole organization.*

*When you manage grants for relatively short periods of time, you
face this same risk of poor commitment to people and processes. The
commitment to effective and efficient grant management can pay
dividends in terms of creating future funding opportunities and
developing a strong positive reputation in the grants community to
recruit and keep accomplished grants professionals.*

Examples of Direct Costs

Let's move on to some examples of direct costs when you are
managing a federal program or project.

The OMB Super Circular includes over fifty examples of
costs and the cost treatments associated with them, in the
General Provisions for Selected Items of Cost section. It is a
good resource if you have further questions about the proper
treatment of a particular cost.

The list of costs that can be included in the direct cost category can be diverse.

The first point to remember in reviewing direct costs is to make sure they really are direct costs. Remember, to be direct costs, the costs must be identified specifically with a particular final cost objective, such as a project or program.

The list of costs that can be included in the direct cost category can be diverse. Some of the primary types of direct costs are:

- Personnel costs
- Materials and supplies
- Equipment that typically has a useful life of more than one year and a cost of more than $5,000
- Training costs for direct employees
- Travel costs for direct employees

Some examples of special types of direct costs include:

- Medical malpractice insurance
- Specialized service facilities

Let's look at each of these examples in further depth.

Personnel Costs

Direct personnel costs include compensation of employees for the time spent working specifically or directly on the performance of the federal award. Personnel costs for direct employees generally include reasonable wages and fringe benefits.

Reasonable wages mean those wages that are consistent with the wages paid for similar work within the organization and are comparable to wages paid in the labor market that the federal award recipient competes in for the kind of employees involved.

Institutions of higher education may have personnel costs that include reasonable costs for activities directly related to the sponsored agreement, such as:

- Attending special lectures
- Writing reports and articles regarding the sponsored research
- Consulting with colleagues
- Attending related meetings and conferences

Materials and Supplies

Direct materials and supplies include materials, supplies, and fabricated parts needed to perform the activities of the federal award. The direct cost is net of any applicable credits such as discounts and rebates. Materials and supplies typically include the cost of incoming shipping charges to get the materials and supplies to the federal award recipient.

Equipment

Direct costs for equipment generally include only special-purpose equipment. Special-purpose equipment is equipment used for research, medical, scientific, or other technical activities. Unless approved in advance by the awarding agency, direct costs would not include general-purpose equipment such as office equipment, furnishings, IT systems, and vehicles.

The goal is to include only costs that are directly tied to a specific final cost objective. General-purpose equipment can be used to support multiple cost objectives. Therefore, the purchase of general-purpose equipment cannot be considered direct cost without the prior approval of the awarding agency.

Training Costs

Training costs include:

- The cost of training materials
- Straight-time wages for employees attending the training
- Instructor costs, such as training fees and travel

To be included in direct costs, the purpose of the training should be to increase the vocational effectiveness of the direct cost trainees.

Travel Costs

Travel costs for direct employees include the cost of transportation, lodging, and subsistence, such as meals and incidentals. When using commercial airlines, the airfare must be coach or equivalent, with few exceptions. Any exceptions must be justified and documented for the agency.

Travel costs typically follow the charging practice of the employees incurring the travel costs. In other words, if the employee is charging his or her time as a direct cost, the travel expenses would also be direct costs.

Medical Liability Insurance

Direct costs can often include specialty areas.
The first example is medical liability insurance. Medical liability insurance, also called medical malpractice insurance, is allowed as direct cost, but only if the sponsored research involves human subjects.

If the costs involve multiple sponsored projects, the allocation of the direct costs for the medical liability insurance follows the insurer's risk allocation between the various projects.

Specialized Service Facilities

Specialized service facilities are highly complex or specialized facilities operated by an institution, such as wind tunnels, reactors, and super computers.

If the costs are material or significant, the use of these facilities must be directly charged to the sponsored agreement that benefited from the facilities. The costs must be based on either the actual use of the services, or some other acceptable allocation method.

 **Key Concepts**

• Many examples of direct costs are contained in 2 CFR Part 200.

• To qualify as a direct cost, the cost must be identifiable with a particular direct activity of an award or other final cost objective.

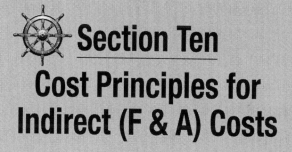 **Section Ten**

Cost Principles for Indirect (F & A) Costs

*W*hen you ask for funding to cover operating costs for your grant office, you will likely be disappointed in the lack of enthusiastic support. Indirect costs and other forms of administrative costs just don't have the sex appeal of direct costs i.e. working directly on the project or program. (For example, when I worked on a scientific research grant, the office had images of the scientists flying in helicopters over the polar regions shown conspicuously everywhere, but not a single picture of an accounts-payable clerk entering an expense report or helicopter invoice...)

So if you are you wondering how to sell the need for sufficient indirect support staff to funding agencies and donors? It's actually pretty simple. Move your focus from the transaction-based need to the safety and security of the funding dollars. Build on an assurance of strong internal controls that protect the funds so they can serve the public purpose that is intended.

Overview of Topics

In this section, we'll we'll walk through four main areas:

- The basics of indirect costs
- How indirect costs are allocated to various cost objectives
- Indirect cost negotiation and approval
- Examples of indirect costs incurred by your organization

At the end of this section, you should recognize and understand:

- The components of indirect costs
- How to calculate an indirect cost rate
- The process for negotiation and approval of an indirect cost rate for a federal award recipient
- Examples of indirect costs that may be incurred by a federal award recipient

Chapter 1

 # Indirect Cost Basics

J ndirect costs can get a bad rap from program and project staff who views the indirect staff in an adversarial role. In fact, even the best-managed program needs support staff to recruit and hire program staff, purchase needed goods and services, and pay invoices.

But indirect staff can do more by moving from being grant police to being valued partners with the grant staff, assisting the program in meeting performance objectives.

Basics of Indirect Costs

In this chapter we will explore the following topics:

- Indirect cost components
- The cost treatment for minor amounts of cost
- The requirements for consistency in cost treatment between indirect and direct costs
- The major groupings of indirect costs

Indirect Cost Components

According to the 2 CFR Part 200, indirect costs must be allowable. For costs to be allowable, they must first pass the hurdle of being reasonable and allocable. Next, costs must not be limited or excluded by federal cost principles regulations. The federal award recipient must demonstrate that it applies policies uniformly to all activities, not just federal awards.

Allowable costs must be adequately documented. Finally, to be considered indirect costs, the costs must be incurred for joint or common objectives.

Indirect costs generally can't be easily identified with a particular final cost objective, such as a project or program. Indirect costs are frequently thought of as costs for support or administrative services. The determining factor in distinguishing a direct cost from an indirect cost is the identification of the cost with the federal award, rather than with the goods and services involved. Examples of indirect costs include such items as accounting, human resources, and purchasing. Indirect costs may also include costs for executive officers and their support staff.

Minor Amounts

The OMB Super Circular allows federal award recipients to treat minor amounts of direct costs as indirect costs for reasons of practicality, as long as this cost treatment is consistently applied to all types of awards. The goal is consistency of cost treatment, and not unfairly moving costs between cost categories.

Cost Treatment Consistency

Federal cost principles state that if a federal award recipient classifies costs as indirect costs, they may not also classify costs incurred for the same purpose, in like circumstances, as direct costs. The goal is to not have federal award recipients artificially moving costs between direct- and indirect costs categories. For example, as a federal award recipient, if you have two employees working in like circumstances for identical purposes, you are prohibited from classifying one of the employees as direct labor and one as indirect labor.

The regulations do recognize that a major project may explicitly require and budget for administrative or clerical services that can be identified directly with the project. In this type of circumstance, the services may be allowed as direct costs.

Indirect Cost Groupings

There are two main groupings or pools of indirect costs covered in 2 CFR Part 200:

- Facilities costs
- Administration costs

This is why you sometimes hear indirect costs referred to as F & A costs. Note that the federal award recipient is required to separate these two groups of indirect costs if the federal award recipient receives more than $10 million in federally funded direct costs per fiscal year.

The facilities costs pool includes incurred costs for items such as the building, general-purpose equipment, capital improvements, and depreciation or use allowances. Facilities costs can include operations and maintenance costs and certain types of interest on facility-related costs.

The administrative costs grouping or pool includes general administration and general expenses, such as the director's office, accounting, and personnel. The administrative pool is also the catch-all grouping for indirect costs that don't fit into the facilities category.

 **Key Concepts**

- Indirect costs typically include shared or common support and administrative costs.

- Indirect costs may include minimal amounts of direct costs, provided the cost treatment is consistently applied across the Federal award.

- Costs must receive consistent cost treatment. If costs are incurred for the same purpose and in like circumstances, they must be treated consistently as either indirect costs or direct costs.

- Indirect costs are typically divided into two main categories: facilities costs and administration costs.

Chapter 2

Indirect Cost Allocation

*T*he writing is on the wall, so get ready. There will be continued downward pressure on indirect cost rates from funding agencies. Think of it this way…if a federal agency can pay a 10% indirect cost rate to a grantee without having to go through the long and painful indirect cost-rate proposal review and negotiation, why would the agency choose to award a grant to an grantee with a 20% indirect cost rate agreement?

Allocation Basics

Indirect cost allocations are usually expressed as either a percentage or square footage charge, as in the case of a facilities allocation. Indirect cost rates are calculated by dividing the total allowable indirect costs by the modified total direct cost base to determine the indirect cost-rate percentage.

Finding the Right Cost Driver

The goal in indirect cost allocation is to match the best cost driver to the allocation base used in the indirect cost allocation. For example, facilities costs are typically allocated to the square footage used by the various projects or programs and support staff. In this case, the square footage used may be a better cost driver than the program spending or labor costs.

Likewise, indirect costs are usually allocated over the cost driver of Modified Total Direct Costs (MTDC) rather than total direct costs. The goal is to match the cost driver with the benefits provided by the indirect cost pool. MTDC is designed to minimize the distorting effects of certain items such as large subawards or equipment purchases included in the direct cost base.

Indirect cost allocations should follow a traceable cause-and-effect relationship or a logical and reasoned approach if neither the cause nor the effect of the relationship is determinable.

Simplified Indirect Cost Rate Example

Let's imagine, in a simplified example, that your total indirect costs are $1 million and your MTDC is $10 million. That ratio would return an indirect cost-rate percentage of ten percent.

- Indirect costs = $1,000,000
- MTDC = $10,000,000
- Indirect cost-rate percentage = $1,000,000 / $10,000,000 = 10%

Purpose of Indirect Cost Allocation

It is worth noting that indirect cost allocations are not a tax on the direct cost programs. The indirect cost allocation is simply a method for spreading support costs to the cost objectives or programs that benefit from them. The allocation of indirect costs to a direct cost base must not be to avoid funding deficiencies or to avoid restrictions placed by the terms and conditions of the award or other federal regulations. However, federal cost principles do permit an allocation of indirect costs to a direct cost base for the purpose of shifting costs allowable under two or more awards in accordance with federal statutes, regulations, or the terms and conditions of the award.

Common Allocation Methods

Some common methods used to allocate indirect costs to federal awards include:

- Simplified allocation method
- Multiple allocation base method
- Direct allocation method
- Special indirect cost rates method

An allocation method is the process for taking a category or pool of indirect costs and spreading those costs over some direct cost base. Generally, the direct cost base that is used for allocating indirect costs is the Modified Total Direct Cost base.

Depending on the number of major functions and the manner in which they benefit from indirect costs, there could be multiple indirect cost pools and cost bases, or just one of each.

Now let's look at the allocation methods in further detail.

Simplified Allocation Method

This method is used when there is only one major function, or when all the major functions at the organization benefit from the indirect costs grouping in approximately the same degree.

For example, if a federal award recipient has multiple awards, but they all receive support from the accounting, purchasing, and other support functions to approximately the same degree or in similar proportion to their respective direct cost bases, the federal award recipient may be able to use the simplified allocation method.

Multiple Allocation Base Method

This method is used when the major functions benefit from indirect costs in varying degrees.

For example, if a federal award recipient has one award that represents ten percent of the direct cost base, but consumes ninety percent of the indirect cost pool benefits, it wouldn't be appropriate to allocate indirect costs in the same manner to the remaining awards, which represent ninety percent of the direct cost base, but only ten percent of the indirect cost benefit.

You may need the multiple allocation base method when:

Chart 1: Multiple Allocation Base Method

Direct Cost Base	Indirect Cost Benefit
Award 1: 10% of direct cost base spending	Award 1: 90% of indirect cost benefits
Award 2: 90% of direct cost base spending	Award 2: 10% of of indirect cost benefits

In this example, we would attempt to better match the benefit received by the major functions by creating multiple indirect cost groupings and multiple Modified Total Direct Cost bases.

Direct Allocation Method

This method may be used by some non-profit organizations when all costs are treated as direct costs except for general expenses and fund-raising costs. All joint costs, such as facilities costs, are directly pro-rated to each category and to each award, using the cost base most appropriate to the joint cost being pro-rated. This method may be allowed, provided the joint costs are pro-rated using a base that accurately measures the benefits received.

Special Indirect Cost Rates

For the most part, the same indirect cost rate is applied to all awards, but in some circumstances a single indirect cost rate may not be appropriate. This condition can occur when the level of indirect costs needed to support a particular award is significantly different from the rest of the activities of an organization for the major functions of the organization. Factors considered for special indirect cost rates include the level of administrative support needed, the technical skills required, and the physical location of the work.

Special Allocation Methods For Governmental Units

The OMB, in response to the National Performance Review's recommendations, encourages federal agencies to work with governmental units and explore fee-for-service arrangements as a replacement for cost-reimbursement plans. This policy seeks to reduce the administrative burden of maintaining systems for charging costs to federal programs and preparing and approving cost-allocation plans. It is hoped that this approach will increase the governmental unit's administrative efficiency.

Three main methods allocate indirect costs to federal awards:

- Central services cost allocation
- Public assistance cost allocation
- Indirect cost rate proposal

Central Services Cost Allocation Plan

Central service costs can include allocated or billed central services. Examples of allocated central services include accounting or purchasing services allocated to the benefiting departments, on a reasonable basis. An example of billed central services is when the benefiting department or agency is billed on an individual fee-for-service or similar basis. Examples of billed central service may include use of computer-processing time, transportation services, or fringe-benefit costs.

The central service cost-allocation method is used when centralized services are provided by the governmental unit and need to be assigned to individual operating agencies within that governmental unit. Typically, agreements would be in place between these individual operating agencies and the federal government. The central service cost-allocation plan allocates a fair share of indirect costs to the individual operating agencies and to the federal awards they support.

The process for submitting a central service cost-allocation plan is contained in Appendix C of 2 CFR Part 225. This method involves identifying and assigning central service costs on a reasonable and consistent basis. The regulations mandate specific documentation that must be submitted with the plan and retained to support the indirect costs. The regulations also include a requirement for the plan to be certified by a governmental unit official.

The central service cost-allocation method generally results in a cost-allocation plan being negotiated and approved for a future fiscal year on a fixed with carry-forward basis. This means that any differences between the costs estimated in the plan and the actual costs incurred would be adjusted in a future period.

Public Assistance Cost Allocation Plan

A public-assistance cost-allocation plan consists of various documents, including a narrative describing the procedures for use in identifying, measuring, and allocating administrative costs incurred for programs run by state public-assistance agencies. Some types of federal programs that may use public-assistance cost-allocation plans include:

Temporary assistance to needy families, such as:

- Medicaid
- Food stamps
- Child-support enforcement
- Adoption assistance
- Foster-care and social-services block grants

As part of its stewardship requirements, the Department of Health and Human Services has published requirements for use by state public-assistance agencies in developing, documenting, submitting, and negotiating public-assistance cost-allocation plans. These guidelines can be found in subpart E of 45 CFR Part 95.

The cost-allocation-plan process includes evaluation of proposed cost groupings as well as review of proposed allocation bases. The federal government also seeks assurance that the plan is implemented as approved through the use of reviews and audits of the program and governmental unit records. In the case of a dispute over the appropriateness of charges to the federal program, the governmental unit may need to credit subsequent claims or even refund the disallowed costs.

Indirect Cost Rate Proposal

An indirect cost rate proposal may be used to allocate indirect costs that originate in each department or agency of the governmental unit carrying out the federal award. The indirect costs can include centralized government services that could be distributed to the various departments under a central service cost-allocation plan. An indirect cost rate proposal would not be used by federal programs that are covered under a public-assistance cost-allocation plan.

The three types of indirect cost allocation methods discussed earlier could be used to allocate indirect costs to federal awards under an indirect cost rate proposal include:

- The simplified allocation method
- The multiple-allocation base method
- The special indirect cost rates method

Special Allocation Methods for Institutions of Higher Education (IHE)

Institutions of higher education, in determining indirect cost allocations (which will typically be called F & A allocations at IHE's) should follow a traceable cause-and-effect relationship or a logical and reasoned approach if neither the cause nor the effect of the relationship is determinable.

Base Period for Calculation

The base period used for calculating the F & A cost pool is the period in which the costs are incurred. It generally coincides with the fiscal year of the institution. The institution should also give thought to the selection of the period to avoid inequities in the cost distribution.

Major Functions for Cost Allocation

Institutions have four major functions that have F & A costs spread to them:

- Instruction
- Organized research
- Other sponsored activities (both federally sponsored and non-federally sponsored)
- Other institutional activities

Let's look at each of these major functions in greater depth: The term "instruction" includes activities such as teaching and training. Teaching and training incorporates for-credit and non-credit courses, regular academic offerings, and other divisions, such as summer school and extension services. Instruction also includes departmental research and other university research when that research is not included in the organized research major function.

Organized research includes all research and development that is tracked through the use of budgets and other means. This major function includes all sponsored research, as well as training individuals in research techniques. This form of research training is included in organized research when the training activities use the same facilities as other research and development activities and the costs aren't already included in the instruction major function. Finally, organized research includes university research that is funded internally by the institution.

Other sponsored activities include sponsored programs and projects that involve the performance of work by the institution, but are not instruction or organized research. Some examples of other sponsored activities include such things as health-service projects and other community-service programs.

Finally, the other institutional activities function is the catch-all category for everything that is <u>not</u>:

- Instruction
- Organized research
- Other sponsored activities
- Specialized service facilities, such as wind tunnels
- F & A cost activities

Remember that these major functions of the institution are going to have F & A costs spread <u>to</u> them, so it makes sense that we would not also include F & A costs in a major function.

Some examples of activities that could be included in the "other institutional activities" major function would be:

- Residence halls and other housing facilities
- Hospitals and clinics
- Intercollegiate athletics
- Public museums

And this "other" category also includes unallowable costs that could not be charged to the sponsored agreement.

Examples of Allocations

Let's looks at some examples of facilities and indirect cost allocations:

Example of Facilities Allocation

Let's start with an example where it has been determined that square footage is the best cost driver to allocate common-facilities costs. In this example, we have $100,000 of common-facilities costs. We have three groups of final cost objectives for allocation. The first group uses fifty percent of the square footage and the second and third groups each use twenty-five percent of the remaining space.

- Common facilities costs = $100,000
- Group #1 uses 50% of the facilities square footage
- Group #2 uses 25% of the facilities square footage
- Group #3 uses 25% of the facilities square footage

Next we will look at how we would allocate the common-facilities costs. In this example, we multiply the $100,000 by the percentage of the square footage used; in order to determine how much of the common–facilities cost is charged to each final cost objective.

For the first final-cost objective, we multiply the $100,000 by fifty percent and the resulting $50,000 is allocated or charged to that project, program, or department. Note that the final-cost objectives could be direct cost programs or indirect cost functions, such as the accounting department.

Group #1 Example:

- Common-facilities costs = $100,000 x 50% = $50,000 allocated to group #1

Remaining Groups:

- Group #2 common-facilities costs = $100,000 x 25% = $25,000 allocated to group #2
- Group #3 common-facilities costs = $100,000 x 25% = $25,000 allocated to group #3

Example of Indirect Cost Allocation

Next, let's look at an example of how indirect costs may be allocated. In this example, we have $1 million of indirect costs and $10 million of MTDC. MTDC is composed of two awards: award #1 has incurred $6 million of modified total direct costs and award #2 has incurred $4 million of modified total direct costs. In this example, the indirect cost rate is calculated by dividing the total allowable indirect costs by the Modified Total Direct Cost base. When allowable indirect costs are $1 million and MTDC are $10 million, the indirect cost-rate percentage is 10%. For every dollar of Modified Total Direct Costs, ten cents of indirect costs is attached to the dollar of MTDC.

- Indirect costs = $1,000,000
- Modified Total Direct Costs (MTDC) = $10,000,000
- Award #1 incurs $6,000,000 of MTDC (60%)
- Award #2 incurs $4,000,000 of MTDC (40%)
- Indirect cost rate = $1,000,000 / $10,000,000 = 10%
- For $1 of MTDC, $0.10 of indirect costs attaches to MTDC and to the project or program

In this example, award #1 has $6 million of MTDC; $6 million multiplied by 10% equals $600,000 of indirect costs allocated to award #1.

- Award #1 $6,000,000 MTDC x 10% = $600,000 of indirect costs allocated to award #1.

Another way to look at this same example is that since award #1 represents 60% of the MTDC, then 60% of the total indirect costs belong to award #1. In this example, sixty percent of the $1 million of indirect costs equals $600,000.

- Award #1 MTDC = $6,000,000/$10,000,000; Total MTDC = 60% of total MTDC
- 60% x $1,000,000 total indirect costs = $600,000 of indirect costs allocated to award #1

 **Key Concepts**

- There are different methods for allocating indirect costs to the direct costs.
- The goal is to match the cost driver to the best allocation method.
- Most indirect cost allocation methods are expressed as a percentage of the Modified Total Direct Cost (MTDC) or as a rate per cost driver, such as square footage used.

Chapter 3

Indirect Cost Rates

*O*ne of the goals of the new grant management regulations is to reduce the administrative burden for grant recipients. At this moment, the change in the grant guidance may not feel like a reduction in your workload, but don't lose hope.

You just have to do a little digging to find some gems in the new 2 CFR Part 200 for federal awards, in the form of new options for indirect costs rates. Let's walk through the basics…

Cognizant Agency

Indirect cost rates are developed in conjunction with your "cognizant agency." A cognizant agency is the federal agency responsible for negotiating and approving indirect cost rates on behalf of all federal agencies. The cognizant agency sets the indirect cost rate that the federal award recipient will use for all of their federal awards.

The cognizant agency is usually the federal agency that has the largest dollar value of awards with the federal award recipient. Note that the cognizant agency stays assigned to the federal award recipient indefinitely unless a major shift in award funding for the federal award recipient occurs.

De minimis vs. Negotiated Rates

The OMB Super Circular distinguishes two main categories of indirect cost rates: "de minimis" and "negotiated." The de minimis indirect cost rate is a standard ten percent of

Modified Total Direct Costs (MTDC). This rate requires no indirect cost proposal and is available to certain federal award recipients that have never received a negotiated indirect cost rate. The de minimis indirect cost rate can be used indefinitely or until such time as the federal award recipient decides to apply for a negotiated indirect cost rate.

Negotiated indirect cost rates are those arising from negotiations between the federal award recipient and the cognizant agency. Unlike de minimis indirect cost rates, which require no action to initiate, negotiated indirect cost rates require the submission of a proposal and subsequent approval by the cognizant agency. Once approved, both the cognizant agency and the federal award recipient execute an agreement confirming the rate, which is made available to and honored by all concerned federal agencies.

Types of Negotiated Rates

Federal cost principles recognize four main types of negotiated indirect cost rates:

- Predetermined rate
- Fixed rate
- Provisional or "billing" rate
- Final rate

Predetermined Rate

Let's look at some of the similarities and differences among these four types of negotiated rates. In the case of the predetermined rate, the rate is used for a specified current or future period. The predetermined rate is based on an estimate of costs, hence the name "predetermined." The predetermined rate is not subject to adjustment and any surplus or shortage is borne by the federal award recipient.

Fixed Rate

The fixed rate is also for a specified current or future period of time and is based on an estimate of costs. Any difference, however, between the estimated costs and the actual cost is carried forward to adjust a future rate.

Provisional or "Billing" Rate

This type of rate is designed to be used during a specified period of funding. Frequently, provisional rates are expressed as a "not to exceed" provisional rate. This rate is also called the "billing rate" because a federal award recipient may bill the federal award for indirect costs based on this provisional rate. The biggest difference between the provisional rate and the other two types of rates mentioned above (the pre-determined and the fixed rate) is that the federal award recipient must go back and make adjustments to the provisional rate to bring the amounts billed in line with the final rate representing the actual costs.

Final Rate

The final rate is used to actualize a specified past period. It is based on the actual costs for that period and not an estimate. Once the rate is finalized it cannot be adjusted. Typically, an organization may have a provisional rate and once the specified period is over the rate will be recalculated with actual costs to determine the final rate.

Chart 2: Comparison of Rate Types

Type of Rate	Period Covered	Based On	Subject to Adjustment
Predetermined	Specified current or future period	Estimate of costs	No
Fixed	Specified current or future period	Estimate of costs	Carry forward adjustments to future rate
Provisional or "Billing"	Specified period of funding	Estimate of costs	Yes, pending establishment of final rate
Final	Specified past period	Actual costs	No

Negotiation Process

Step 1: The first step in negotiating an indirect cost rate with the federal award recipient's cognizant agency is to submit an indirect cost rate proposal to the agency. This proposal should include documentation prepared by the federal award recipient to substantiate the claims for reimbursement of indirect costs. The proposal should be consistent with the goal of matching the cost drivers to the appropriate indirect cost pools.

Step 2: Once the indirect cost rate proposal is received by the cognizant agency, there will usually be a review and negotiation of the proposal between the agency and the federal award recipient.

Step 3: When the negotiations are completed, the cognizant agency will generate a written indirect cost rate agreement for both the agency and the recipient to formally accept.

Step 4: Once the written agreement is finalized, the cognizant agency has the responsibility to distribute the finalized indirect cost rate agreement to other federal agencies as needed.

Negotiation Time Frame

The OMB Super Circular states that the first time the federal award recipient submits an indirect cost rate proposal to its cognizant agency, the proposal should be submitted immediately after the federal award recipient is notified of its federal award, but no later than three months after the award's effective date. If the federal award recipient already has an established indirect cost rate, the federal award recipient must submit new proposals within six months following the close of each fiscal year.

 **Key Concepts**

- The federal award recipient's indirect cost rate proposal is negotiated with the federal award recipient's cognizant agency.

- There are various types of negotiated indirect costs rates and some of those rates are subject to adjustment once actual costs are determined.

- A de minimis indirect cost rate of 10% of MTDC is available to certain federal award recipients that have never had a negotiated indirect cost rate. The de minimis indirect cost rate requires no indirect cost proposal to the cognizant agency.

- The deadlines for submitting indirect cost rate proposals depend on whether the federal award recipient has previously established indirect cost rates with its cognizant agency.

Chapter 4

Examples of Indirect Costs

Avoid the red-flag areas that are reviewed in determining reasonableness of costs. Remember, actions that unjustifiably increase the costs to the federal government are not considered reasonable, according to the regulations.

Examples of Indirect Costs

The OMB Super Circular includes over fifty examples of costs and their corresponding cost treatment. It is a good resource if you have further questions about the proper treatment of a particular cost. The first point to remember in reviewing indirect costs is to make sure they really are indirect costs. The cost must be incurred for a common or joint objective and not readily identified with a particular final cost objective to be an indirect cost.

Some primary types of indirect costs include:

- General administrative expenses
- Personnel administration costs
- Salaries and expenses of executive officers
- Facilities costs
- Accounting costs

Administrative Expenses

Administrative expenses include reasonable wages and fringe benefits for general clerical or administrative staff. Reasonable wages are consistent with wages paid for similar work within the organization and the costs are comparable to wages paid in the labor market that the federal award recipient competes in and for the kind of employees involved.

Administrative expenses also include general items such as business insurance. For these types of administrative costs to be allowable and included in indirect costs, the costs must be reasonable and consistent with sound business practices.

Personnel Administration

The costs for personnel administration typically include such indirect costs as:

- Staff salaries and related fringe benefits
- Costs of employee-information publications
- Labor-relations costs
- Employee-assistance plans, provided that these costs are consistent with established organizational practices

Executive Officer Costs

Indirect costs for executive officers include such items as reasonable wages and fringe benefits, travel, and other types of subsistence costs for executive officers. The costs must meet the allowable criteria, which includes the costs being considered reasonable and adequately documented.

Facilities Costs

Facilities costs include:

- Facilities staff and related fringe benefits
- Building rent and utilities
- Building security and maintenance, including the staff and related costs
- Depreciation and use allowances, if applicable, for buildings, equipment, and other capital improvements

Note that the calculation of depreciation and use allowances has numerous rules and guidelines and is beyond the scope of this book.

Accounting Costs

Accounting costs include the costs to support audit activities and produce required reports. Indirect costs also typically include accounting staff and related fringe benefits, as well as tax preparation and filing costs.

Key Concepts

- Many examples of indirect costs are contained in 2 CFR Part 200.

- For the most part, to be included in indirect costs, the cost must be incurred for common or joint objectives not readily identified with a particular direct activity of an award.

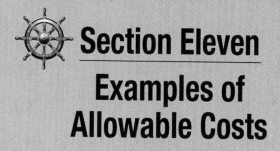 **Section Eleven**

Examples of
Allowable Costs

I recently had a conversation with a dedicated and innovative engineer about how to receive funding for his organization, which builds specially designed 3D printers to create prosthetic hands for children injured by the effects of war and poverty. It is certainly an admirable and exciting program that could transform the lives of some of the most vulnerable and traumatized citizens in diverse areas of the world.

However, he was focused on the cool technology rather than on the young lives that could be dramatically improved, from a place of hopelessness to one of pride and excitement. He failed to recognize that funders care more about programs and people. Simply put, funders want to fund programs that make a difference and change lives for the better.

Overview of Topics

In this section, you'll hear more about four main areas:

- The basics of cost allowability
- Examples of employee related allowable costs
- Examples of facilities and equipment-related allowable costs
- Examples of other types of allowable costs

At the end of this section, you should recognize and understand:

- The components of allowable costs
- Types of employee related allowable costs
- Equipment and facilities-related allowable costs
- Examples of other allowable cost types

Chapter 1

Allowability Basics

*A*llowability includes allocability. This means that costs must be allocable to the award, consistent with the relative benefit received by the federal program. Say what?

Think of it this way. When costs are allocated to an award, the costs must be a realistic amount in line with the benefits the federal award is receiving. For example, if the award needs the support of the indirect cost departments to cover one part-time person processing invoices, it wouldn't be allowable to allocate the cost of three buildings and six indirect staff people to the award.

Basics of Allowability

In this chapter we will explore the following topics:

- The criteria for cost allowability
- The cost treatment between indirect and direct costs and the effect on allowability
- The concept of conditional allowability

Cost Criteria

The OMB Super Circular outlines several conditions for costs to qualify as allowable. First, costs must pass the hurdles of being necessary, reasonable, and allocable. Next, costs must not be limited or excluded by federal cost principles. The costs must also not be used to meet cost-sharing or matching requirements for any other federally financed program in either the current or a prior period. The federal award recipient must demonstrate that it applies policies uniformly to all activities, not just federal award activities. Finally, allowable costs must be adequately documented.

Cost Treatment

Allowable costs can be either direct costs or indirect costs. Direct costs can be attributed to a particular final cost objective, such as a federally funded project or program. Direct costs can also be attributed to non-federally funded activities. These costs are charged directly to the identifiable final cost objective.

Indirect costs are incurred for joint or common objectives. The objectives of the incurred costs cannot be readily identified with a particular final cost objective, such as a project or program. Indirect costs are charged to an indirect cost pool and then allocated to a direct cost base by one of various allocation methods.

Conditional Allowability

The concept of conditional allowability has to do with whether there are conditions that affect the allowability of the costs incurred. In reviewing the various parts of the federal cost-principles in 2 CFR Part 200, you will find very few types of costs that are allowable or unallowable without specific conditions. These conditions may hinge on whether the costs in question are direct or indirect costs, or the specific circumstances related to activities supported by the costs.

The OMB Super Circular cites more than fifty examples of costs and the cost treatment associated with them. It is a good resource if you have further questions about the allowability of a particular cost.

Key Concepts

* For costs to be allowable, the costs must be necessary, reasonable, allocable, with cost treatment uniformly applied, not limited by federal regulation, not used for cost sharing in other federal programs, and sufficiently documented.

* Cost allowability may depend on whether or not the costs are direct or indirect costs, and the specific circumstances surrounding the activities supported by the costs.

Chapter 2

Allowable Employee Related Costs

*D*o you find it difficult to balance your personal responsibilities and contribute successfully to projects and programs funded by federal awards? If your answer is yes, the OMB agrees with you! The new super-circular has made it simpler to support family-friendly leave policies in your fringe benefits.

Common Examples of Employee Related Costs

The OMB Super Circular addresses the following types of employee related allowable costs:

- Employee compensation such as wages and salaries
- Fringe benefits including paid leave
- Employee health and welfare benefits
- Employee travel

Compensation Costs

Employee compensation, also known as compensation for personal services, is defined as:

- All compensation paid or accrued for employees during the period of the award
- This definition includes wages, salaries, and other forms of employee compensation

Note that the definition of compensation for personal services is expanded to include director and executive committee fees.

Compensation for personal services broadly includes not only employee wages, but also fringe benefits and health and welfare costs that may be allocated to employee labor costs.

Compensation for personal services is conditionally allowable, depending on the following circumstances:

- The total compensation must be reasonable when compared to the services provided to the federal award recipient.
- The compensation must conform to established organizational policies. This also applies to the new family-leave benefits.
- The organizational policies must be consistently applied to both federal and non-federal activities.

Compensation for personal services is usually judged to be reasonable when the following criteria are met:

- The wages paid are consistent with wages paid for similar activities performed by other organizational functions
- The compensation must be comparable to similar work in the labor market that the federal award recipient competes in and for the kind of employee being utilized

There are several red flags that federal award recipients should be aware of, related to compensation. Red flags that may draw additional scrutiny from the awarding or cognizant agency include compensation paid to members of the organization receiving the federal award, trustees, directors, associates, officers, or the immediate families thereof.

The federal government may also look deeper into changes in the compensation policy of the federal award recipient that result in a substantial increase in compensation for all or some employees. The agency may take particular exception if the substantial increase happens concurrently with an increase in the federal award.

Fringe Benefits

Compensation for personal services broadly includes not only employee wages, but also fringe benefits that may be allocated to employee labor costs. Fringe benefits include items such as paid leave, pension costs, and common types of health insurance.

For costs to be allowable fringe benefits, the company must consistently apply the benefits to both federal and non-federal activities. This also applies to the new family-leave benefits contained in 2 CFR Part 200 designed to support women in the STEM fields.

Employee Health and Welfare Costs

Employee health and welfare costs include such items as:

- Employee informational publications
- Health or first-aid clinics
- Recreational activities with employees
- Employee counseling services
- Other similar types of activities

The non-federal entity should be aware that entertainment costs are unallowable, and should also be clear on the fine-line distinction between employee recreational activities and entertainment costs.

For employee health and welfare costs to be allowable, they must be consistent with established practices or customs of the organization.

Costs incurred to support the improvement of working conditions; employer-employee relations, employee morale, and employee performance are usually allowable. These costs are typically allocated to all activities of the organization, not just the federal award.

Employee Travel

Travel costs are defined as the costs for transportation, lodging, and subsistence, such as meals and various incidentals. To qualify as allowable costs, the employee must be in travel status for the federal award recipient while conducting official business.

Travel costs are allowable subject to specific rules regarding reasonableness. For example, an employee's travel costs must be reasonable and consistent with a federal award recipient's written travel policy.

Another condition for allowability is that commercial air travel (with some exceptions) must be coach or an equivalent fare. Any exceptions must be justified and documented to the agency.

Travel costs can either represent actual costs, per-diem costs, or a combination method. The selected method, however, must be used consistently for the entire trip and not applied selectively to certain days. The selected method must charge both federal and non-federal activities in like manner. In other words, the method for recording travel costs should be consistent among all travel activities of the federal award recipient. The federal government does not want a different and potentially more expensive method applied to federal awards.

Finally, let's look at travel costs for trustees and directors of the federal award recipient. Costs for trustee or director travel are conditionally allowable and include such costs as transportation, lodging, subsistence, and related items. While these individuals may not qualify as employees, they are subject to the same restrictions as employees regarding travel costs.

Other Employee Related Costs

Let's move on to some other costs related to employees. In this part we will explore the following topics:

- Training costs
- Memberships, subscriptions, and professional activity costs
- Costs for page charges in professional journals

Training Costs

Training costs are costs for the preparation and maintenance of a program of instruction for the employees.

Training costs typically include items such as:

- The cost of training materials
- Straight-time wages for employees attending the training
- Instructor costs, such as training fees and travel

Training and education costs for employee development are allowable.

Memberships, Subscriptions, and Professional Costs

Memberships, subscriptions, and professional activity costs are assumed to be costs in support of business, technical, or professional organizations. These costs are generally allowable for items such as:

- Subscriptions to business, professional, or technical periodicals
- Membership in civic or community organizations, provided the cognizant agency gives prior approval

Page Charges

Finally, professional-journal page charges are typically allowable costs if the costs are a necessary part of the federally sponsored research work. To qualify as an allowable cost, page costs must be for publications reporting on work supported by the federal government and consistently charged to all research papers published, not just to federally sponsored authors.

 # Key Concepts

- Examples of many types of allowable costs related to employees are provided in 2 CFR Part 200.

- Many of the items have very specific restrictions on their allowability, but generally, costs must be reasonable and follow organizational policies for employees and employee related costs.

- The federal government wants to ensure costs are applied to awards consistently with other non-federal activities.

Chapter 3

Allowable Facilities and Equipment Costs

hink that you can spend grant funds and then be done with it? Like the kid that won't leave home after college, facilities and equipment purchases is one area of grant management that has many twists and turns, ranging from how the property is titled to what approvals may be necessary for the costs to be allowed by your funding agency. And the responsibilities don't stop just because the period of performance has ended.

Allowable Costs for Equipment and Facilities

There are a number of nuances to be aware of when looking at allowable costs for equipment and facilities. In this chapter we look at the classification of capital expenditures as well as some other examples of allowable costs for facilities, equipment.

Classification of Capital Expenditures

Equipment and other capital expenditures are defined as tangible personal property, including information technology systems, having a useful life of more than one year and a per-unit net-acquisition cost that is greater than the lesser of the federal award recipient's capitalization level, or $5,000. "Net acquisition cost" means the acquisition cost, less any applicable credits such as rebates or discounts. The net acquisition costs may also include costs to deliver the equipment (or deliver any other capital expenditure) and initiate its use, assuming the treatment of these costs is consistent with the treatment of other similar costs.

Equipment is specifically defined as the lesser of the federal award recipient's capitalization level or $5,000. If the organization has a capitalization level lower than $5,000, all equipment meeting these criteria must be treated as a capital expenditure – even if the cost is under $5,000.

Equipment: Special Purpose vs. General Purpose

Equipment purchased by Federal awards is typically divided into two categories: special purpose equipment and general purpose equipment. Special purpose equipment includes equipment which is used for research, medical, scientific, and other similar technical activities. General purpose equipment is defined as equipment whose use is not limited to special purposes. The Federal government does not want the award to pay for general purpose equipment that could be shared with activities other than those included in the Federal award. For this reason, Federal regulations treat special purpose equipment different than general purpose equipment.

Equipment: Direct Costs vs. Indirect Costs

Let's look at the cost treatment for these two types of equipment. Special purpose equipment is generally allowable as a direct cost to the federal award. Normally, the federal award recipient must have the prior approval of the awarding agency to purchase equipment costing over $5,000. The regulations also state that general purpose equipment should not be charged as a direct cost to the federal award without prior approval of the awarding agency.

Now let's look at equipment and other capital expenditures and the cost treatment for indirect costs. The purchase of equipment and other capital expenditures are generally an unallowable charge to the award. Instead, the costs for the indirect purchase of equipment and other capital expenditures should be recouped through depreciation charges or a use allowance. Special purpose equipment is not charged to the indirect cost pool. Special purpose equipment by its very nature should be attributable to a final cost objective, and therefore would not meet the criteria for inclusion as an indirect cost.

Other Examples of Facilities and Equipment Costs

Specifically, we will explore the following topics in this part:

- Depreciation charges and use allowances
- Rental costs for buildings and equipment
- Repair and maintenance costs
- Plant security costs
- Costs related to rearrangement, alteration, and reconversion of the federal award recipient's facilities

Depreciation Charges and Use Allowances

Depreciation charges and use allowances are defined in the regulations as methods for compensating the federal award recipient for the use of buildings, capital improvements, and equipment. While depreciation and use allowances are generally allowable costs, specific rules apply. Depreciation charges and use allowances must be supported by adequate property records. Additionally, a physical inventory must be taken at least every two years to verify the capital assets related to the depreciation charges and use allowances.

Rental Costs

Specific cost-treatment rules apply to rental costs. Operating leases such as month-to-month leases, where the federal award recipient does not retain ownership, may qualify as allowable costs. On the other hand, the federal award recipient may need to treat a capital lease as a capital asset purchase. Federal agencies critically scrutinize transactions than don't have full and open competition (often called less-than-arms-length transactions) related to rental and lease arrangements.

Generally, rental costs for buildings and equipment are conditionally allowable, provided:

- The costs are reasonable when compared with similar properties in similar market conditions and weighed against available alternatives
- The cost for the rental may not exceed the arm's-length lease costs, if applicable
- The federal award recipient should be prepared to demonstrate that the cost to rent or lease does not exceed the cost the federal award recipient would have incurred had it purchased the property

Repairs and Maintenance

Repair and maintenance costs include costs to keep the building or equipment in efficient operating condition. If the expenditure adds to the permanent value or appreciably extends the useful life of the property, the expenditure should be treated as a capital expenditure and not as repairs and maintenance. For example, replacing a flat tire on a vehicle is considered a repair or maintenance cost to keep the property in efficient operational condition. On the other hand, replacing the engine on a car with 100,000 miles on it will appreciably extend the useful life of the property, thereby qualifying as a capital expenditure. Repair and maintenance costs are generally allowable costs chargeable to a federal award if the costs are incurred for necessary maintenance, repair, or upkeep of the property.

Plant Security

Typically, plant and homeland security costs are allowable if they are necessary and reasonable expenses to protect facilities, personnel, and work products. Plant and homeland security costs may include such items as security-personnel wages, uniforms, security consultants, and related items, such as security barriers.

Rearrangement

Rearrangement, alteration, and reconversion costs are related to the rearrangement or alteration of facilities. These costs can include restoring or rehabilitating facilities back to the approximate condition prior to the start of the federal award. Rearrangement, alteration, and reconversion costs are typically allowable costs if they are related to normal and ordinary rearrangement, alteration, or reconversion of the facilities. If special or unusual costs are incurred just for the project or program, they require prior approval of the awarding agency.

 **Key Concepts**

- Federal regulations impose specific regulations related to facilities, equipment, and other types of capital expenditures.

- Different cost treatments for capital expenditures may exist if equipment meets the criteria for special purpose or general purpose equipment and if the property is purchased, rented, or leased.

Chapter 4

 **Other Types of Allowable Costs**

*D*o you believe that it's difficult for employees to participate
in out-of-town seminars while balancing their family
responsibilities? In fact, having the realistic opportunity to attend
external meetings conferences is one of the focus areas cited in
the change in grant management policies. Comments received
by the organization who created the lion's share of the new grant
regulations; the Council on Financial Assistance Reform (COFAR)
showed wide agreement that dependent-care costs were a big
deterrent to women attending scientific symposiums and seminars.
In the desire to promote diversity in the conference population, new
types of allowable costs are included in meetings and conference costs.

Other Examples of Allowable Costs

In this chapter, we will look at the following areas:

- A variety of services provided for the federal award
- The cost treatment for materials and supplies
- Some miscellaneous allowable costs, such as
  participant support and pre-award costs

Service Related Costs

Let's start by looking at the following types of allowable
service costs:

- Professional services costs
- Publishing services
- Transportation services
- Allowable advertising and public relations services

Professional Services

Professional service costs are defined as services rendered by persons who are members of a particular profession or who possess special skills. Examples of professional service costs include fees to pay attorneys, accountants, engineers, and others who possess specialized skills. Professional service costs are conditionally allowable if the costs are not paid to officers or employees of the federal award recipient.

The charges must be reasonable in relation to the services rendered. The services cannot be provided on a contingency basis, where the payment to the professional is contingent upon recovering the costs from the federal government. Additional considerations related to the allowability of costs for professional services include:

- Whether the services could be performed more economically by direct employment rather than contracting with a service firm
- Whether the services are supported by an adequate contract between the federal award recipient and the professional
- The qualifications of the professional and the customary fees charged for these types of services
- Contracting for these services instead of performing the work in-house

Publications and Printing

Publication and printing costs include the cost of printing, distributing, promoting, mailing, and the general handling of printed materials. This category also includes page charges in professional publications, if necessary for the award. Publication and printing costs are generally allowable as direct costs when they can be identified with a particular cost objective. When the particular cost objective cannot be identified, publication and printing costs are allowable as indirect costs.

Transportation Costs

Transportation costs are defined as the costs for freight, express shipment, cartage, and postage related to the delivery of goods purchased and/or delivered. Transportation costs are generally allowable. When the transportation costs can be readily identified with the items involved, the transportation cost can be added to the cost of the item. If the transportation costs can't be readily identified with a specific item, the costs can be included with indirect costs.

The main point is that the federal award recipient should follow a consistent, equitable process in determining where to charge the transportation costs.

Advertising Costs

Advertising costs are defined as advertising media and related administrative costs. Advertising costs can include print media, electronic media, and radio and television advertising. Very limited instances exist when advertising costs qualify as allowable costs, such as when the federal award recipient requires advertising to perform the activities of the award.

Some examples of when advertising may be required include:

- For personnel recruitment, providing the costs meet certain reasonableness criteria, such as the size and color of the advertisement
- To solicit for procurement of goods and services
- To dispose of scrap or surplus material, unless the disposal costs were already determined by the agency

Public Relations Costs

Public relations costs are defined as costs for community relations and activities to maintain the image of the federal award recipient. This description also includes activities to promote understanding and favorable relations with the public. As with advertising costs, there are very few circumstances when public relations costs are allowable; for example:

- When public relations costs are specifically required by the award
- When the costs relate to communicating with the public and the press regarding award activities or accomplishments
- When the communication is necessary to keep the public informed on matters of public concern, such as notices of awards or financial matters

Miscellaneous Allowable Costs

Federal regulations address the following miscellaneous allowable costs:

- Materials and supplies
- Participant support costs
- Meetings and conferences
- Insurance costs

- Pre-award costs
- Termination costs

Materials and Supplies

Materials and supplies costs include those required to perform the activities of the federal award. The cost is net of any applicable credits, such as discounts and rebates. Materials and supplies costs typically include the cost of incoming shipping charges to get the materials and supplies to the federal award recipient. Materials and supplies costs are generally allowable and can be either direct costs or indirect costs.

To be allowable as direct costs, the materials and supplies must actually be used in the performance of the federal award. The OMB Super Circular now classifies computing devices as supplies; therefore, computing devices can be charged as a direct cost even if they are not dedicated solely to the performance of the federal award. If the materials are donated to the federal award recipient to be used in the award, the materials should be used at no cost to the award.

Participant Support Costs

Participant support costs are primarily used to support participants attending conferences and training. The costs are generally allowable as direct costs if the federal award recipient has received prior approval of the awarding agency. Participant support costs include such items as stipends, subsistence allowances, travel costs, and registration fees. Note that participant support costs may be spent for participants or trainees, but not for employees of the federal award recipient.

Meetings and Conferences

Costs for meetings and conferences are generally allowable if the primary purpose is to disseminate information technical in nature. If the meeting or conference meets the primary purpose test, the allowable costs would include meals, transportation, rental or room costs, speaker fees, and other related costs.

Insurance Costs

Insurance costs are generally allowable if required by the award, or if the insurance is carried as part of sound business practices at the non-federal entity. For the purpose of this part of the regulation, insurance costs don't include insurance covered under the definition of fringe benefits, such as employee health insurance.

Pre-Award Costs

Pre-award costs are defined as costs incurred prior to the effective date of the award. The costs must be directly related to the award. Typically, a federal award recipient may incur pre-award costs to comply with a proposed award delivery schedule or the requirements for the period of performance. Pre-award costs may be allowable, provided the costs incurred would have been allowable if incurred during the award period. A federal award recipient must have the written approval of the federal awarding agency for pre-award costs to be allowable.

The OMB Super Circular specifically states that pre-spending on an award is at the recipient's risk. The federal government is not under any obligation to pay pre-award costs if the recipient does not receive the award or receives an amount that is less than expected.

Termination Costs

Occasionally an award may be terminated by the federal agency. This termination may give rise to special costs that wouldn't have been incurred if the award hadn't been terminated.

The non-federal entity is required to make reasonable efforts to minimize costs in the event of the early termination of an award. The regulations recognize that even with the reasonable efforts of the non-federal entity, some costs related to termination of an award may be incurred. Allowable costs can include such items as:

- Reasonable costs for termination of unexpired leases and may include restoration of facilities
- Settlement of outstanding claims such as claims from subcontractors or subrecipients
- Reasonable costs for protection and storage of property belonging to, or purchased by, the federal awarding agency.

As stated previously, the non-federal entity has a duty to minimize the costs related to termination of an award to those that are reasonably necessary and unavoidable.

 **Key Concepts**

- The OMB Super Circular includes many examples of allowable costs.

- Many of these items have very specific rules regarding allowability of costs. The federal award recipient needs to understand the restrictions so costs can be properly classified.

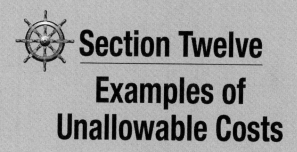

Section Twelve

Examples of Unallowable Costs

Are you new to the world of grant management or are you responsible for checking someone else's spending on a federal grant? You may have heard the term "unallowable costs," but are not sure what exactly that means. You just know it's bad when they slip through in the grant spending.

Unallowable costs are the things that should never, ever, ever see their way into a federal grantee recipient's spending. These are the types of things that keep legions of auditors busy looking for the bad apple in the spending barrel. Even worse, this is the stuff that puts your organization at risk for repayment of grant funds, suspension, and/or debarment from federal grants.

Overview of Topics

In this section, we will look at four main areas:

- The basics of cost unallowability
- Examples of employee related unallowable costs
- Examples of facilities- and equipment-related unallowable costs
- Examples of other unallowable costs that may be incurred by your organization

At the end of this section, you should recognize and understand:

- The components of unallowable costs
- Types of employee related unallowable costs
- Equipment- and facilities-related unallowable costs
- Examples of other unallowable cost types that may be incurred by your organization

Chapter 1

Unallowable Cost Basics

*W*hen an organization includes unallowable costs in costs
charged to its grant(s), dire consequences can result. Those
consequences can include not just the repayment of the amount
spent on unallowable costs, but also fines and penalties, which are
also unallowable to charge the federal award.) Mischarging can even
result in being excluded from future grants. Not only that, but this
kind of behavior by an organization can result in permanent damage
to its reputation.

Unallowable Cost Criteria

The criteria for qualifying costs as unallowable and non-
chargeable to a federal award are the opposite of the
allowable cost criteria. Costs are unallowable if they are
unreasonable or unallocable, even if they meet other criteria.
Costs are unallowable if they are limited or excluded by
federal cost principles. If the federal award recipient applies
its internal policies only to its federal award(s) rather than
uniformly to all activities, or if inadequate documentation
exists to support expenditures, the costs may be unallowable.

Other Considerations

Other considerations exist to determine whether costs are
unallowable:

- Whether procurements are made in full and open competition where required
- Whether transactions involve non-competitive actions such as conflicts of interest or less-than-arm's-length relationships
- Whether the cost is over what an arm's-length transaction would have cost
- Whether the purchase involves prohibited transactions such as fraud, suspension, and debarment and other prohibited business dealings
- Whether the purchase is unnecessary; an item's inclusion in the budget does not make the purchase necessary. The purchase must be necessary for the completion of the objectives of the federal award.

 **Key Concepts**

- Costs may be unallowable if they are unreasonable, unallocable, inconsistently applied, limited by federal regulation, or insufficiently documented.

- Cost unallowability may depend on whether the costs are related to non-competitive practices, conflicts of interest, the necessity of the purchase, and/or whether the transaction was in some other way prohibited.

Chapter 2

Unallowable Employee Related Costs

*W*hen good grants go bad...it makes me sad that I never have far to look for these types of stories, such as a recent story about the Office of the Inspector General finding more than $704,000 in grant funds were either unallowable costs or unsupported questioned costs on a $1.5 million federal award. It's not just the waste of taxpayer funds that makes me angry; it's the waste of potential good that could have been done with those funds, if only the grant had been managed properly!

Examples of Unallowable Employee Related Costs

We will look at the following types of employee related unallowable costs in this chapter, specifically:

- Unallowable fringe benefits
- Other types of employee related unallowable costs

Unallowable Fringe Benefits

Let's look at some examples of when certain employee fringe benefits may be unallowable costs, such as:

- Automobile costs furnished by the federal award recipient
- Certain types of life insurance
- Particular types of severance pay
- Tuition for family members

Automobile Costs

Automobile costs furnished by the federal award recipient for personal use, such as commuting to and from the work location, are normally unallowable, even when reported by the employee as taxable income. This restriction applies to automobile costs that are part of indirect costs or fringe benefits. Note that there may be circumstances when these costs can be allowable as direct costs, provided they are necessary for the performance of the award, and they have the approval of the awarding agency.

Life Insurance

Life insurance costs for coverage on the life of a trustee, officer, and/or other personnel in a similarly responsible position is unallowable if the federal award recipient is named as the beneficiary on the policy. This type of life insurance policy is sometimes called a key man (or woman) policy.

Severance Costs

Severance pay, also referred to as dismissal wages, is a type of compensation payment in addition to regular wages. Severance payments are made by the federal award recipient to an employee facing termination of employment without cause.

The type of severance pay that is an unallowable cost is for mass or abnormal accruals of severance pay. In this type of situation, the nature of the accrual is based on conjecture and the measurement of costs will likely not achieve equity to either the awarding agency or the recipient. In these circumstances, the cost allowability may be considered by the agency on a case-by-case basis.

Golden parachute payments are another type of unallowable severance pay. Golden parachute payments are defined as payments in excess of normal severance pay. They typically occur as a result of a change in ownership, or management control, at an organization. Golden parachute payments are unallowable costs to the federal award.

Severance costs for foreign nationals employed outside the United States are unallowable to the extent that they exceed the customary practice for the federal award recipient in the U.S. In some circumstances, severance payments to a foreign national may be necessary for the performance of the award. In this case, the agency may allow specific payments.

Tuition Costs

The institution may not include costs reflecting tuition benefits for non-employee family members in the fringe benefits charged to the federally-sponsored agreement.

Other Employee Related Unallowable Costs

Let's move on to some other costs related to employees, such as:

- Travel costs
- Goods or services for personal use
- Housing allowances and personal living expenses
- Relocation costs
- Memberships

Employee Travel

Travel costs are defined as the costs for transportation, lodging, and subsistence, such as meals and various incidentals. Costs may be unallowable if the employee is not in travel status for the federal award recipient and conducting official business. Travel costs can be unallowable if the employee's travel costs are not reasonable and consistent with the federal award recipient's written travel policy.

Additionally, if commercial air travel is not coach or an equivalent fare without justification and documentation to the awarding agency, the costs may be unallowable. In the case of non-commercial air travel, costs in excess of the commercial air travel costs could be unallowable.

Travel costs for dependents are also unallowable unless specific circumstances are met where the travel is for six or more months and the federal awarding agency has given prior approval.

Foreign travel costs for direct employees without the prior approval of the awarding agency are unallowable. Please note: the notice of funding opportunity should also list the specific restrictions on foreign travel. When in doubt, consult your funding agency.

Goods and Services for Personal Use

The cost of goods or services for personal use by the federal award recipient's employees is an unallowable cost. Goods and services for personal use are unallowable even if the costs are reported as taxable income to the employee. Some examples include such things as:

- Charging travel costs for family members of an employee
- Personal use of office supplies and shipping services
- Purchasing electronics that are not used in the performance of the federal award

Housing and Personal Living

Housing and personal living expenses include items such as housing allowances, utilities, furnishings, and rent, maintenance, and depreciation charges. Housing and personal living expenses are unallowable costs if treated as indirect costs or fringe benefits, but may be allowable as direct costs if the expenditures are necessary for the performance of the award and approved in advance by the awarding agency.

Relocation Costs

Relocation costs are defined as the costs related to a permanent change of duty assignment. The costs are incurred for a new or existing employee for either an indefinite period or a stated period of at least twelve months. Relocation costs are unallowable if the change in duty assignment is for less than twelve months. Relocation costs are also unallowable if the employee leaves before the twelve-month period expires. In this case, the federal award recipient must reimburse the federal government for any relocation costs that were previously allowed. Relocation costs are unallowable for certain types of excluded costs. Examples of excluded costs could be such items as:

- New home acquisition costs
- Payments on the old home mortgage or any loss on the sale of the old home
- Income tax paid on the relocation reimbursements

Membership Costs

Membership costs unrelated to business, professional or technical purposes are most often unallowable. A primary example of unallowable costs in this area is membership in a country club, social club, dining club, or similar type of activity.

 **Key Concepts**

- Examples of several types of unallowable costs related to employees are included in 2 CFR Part 200.

- Many of the costs have specific restrictions related to unallowability. Generally, costs may be unallowable if they are unreasonable or don't follow the organizational policies for employees and employee related costs.

- The federal government also wants to ensure that costs applied to awards are not unfairly weighted toward federal award activities.

Chapter 3

Unallowable Facility and Equipment Costs

J *did a case study on a news story about the U.S. Department of Housing and Urban Development (HUD) forcing the City of Honolulu to repay nearly $8 million in federal community development block grant funds. Reportedly the city paid eight times more than the fair market value for some of the property purchased by ignoring their own land-use regulations, which resulted in a higher valuation*

Unallowable Costs for Facilities and Equipment

Now we will look at examples of unallowable costs for facilities, equipment, and other types of capital expenditures. Equipment costs and other capital expenditures are defined as tangible personal property, including information technology systems, having a useful life of more than one year and a per-unit net acquisition cost that is greater than the lesser of the federal award recipient's capitalization level or $5,000.

Equipment is specifically defined as the lesser of the federal award recipient's capitalization level or $5,000. Therefore, if the federal award recipient has a capitalization level lower than $5,000, all equipment meeting these criteria must be treated as a capital expenditure, even if the cost is under $5,000.

Equipment: Special Purpose vs. General Purpose

Equipment purchased by federal awards is typically divided into two categories: special purpose equipment and general purpose equipment. Special purpose equipment includes equipment that is used for research, medical, scientific, and other similar technical activities. General purpose equipment is defined as equipment that is not limited to special purposes.

Capital Expenditures: Indirect Costs vs. Direct Costs

Costs for equipment and other capital expenditures are generally unallowable as indirect costs charged to the award. Instead, the costs for indirect purchases of equipment and other capital expenditures would be recouped through depreciation charges or use allowances.

Direct costs for general purpose equipment are generally unallowable because general purpose equipment isn't attributable to a final cost objective and therefore doesn't meet the criteria to be considered direct costs.

Likewise, special purpose equipment is not charged to the indirect cost pool. Special purpose equipment by its very nature is attributable to a final cost objective and therefore doesn't meet the criteria to be considered indirect costs. Specific exceptions may be granted by the agency.

 **Key Concepts**

- Specific regulations exist related to facilities, equipment, and other types of capital expenditures. These regulations can be very complicated.

- Different cost treatments apply to special purpose and general purpose equipment.

Chapter 4

Other Types of Unallowable Costs

*Y*ou may think you have allowable costs to charge to your award, but if prohibited transactions such as fraud, suspension, and debarment, and other prohibited business dealings are involved, the net result will be that the costs are transformed into unallowable costs, even if the transaction meets the rest of the allowable cost criteria. Some additional examples of prohibited business dealings include having conflicts of interest in procurements, and the violation of anti-corruption laws. Be safe, not sorry when it comes spending federal awards.

Other Unallowable Costs

In this chapter, we will look at the following areas of unallowable costs:

- A selection of costs related to various types of meetings
- Advertising, public relations, and marketing costs
- Legal, insurance, and related costs
- Miscellaneous unallowable costs such as donations and losses on sponsored awards

Unallowable Meeting-Related Cost

Let's go back and refresh the definition of meetings and conferences. Costs for meetings and conferences are generally allowable if the primary purpose is to disseminate technical information beyond the federal award recipient and is necessary and reasonable for successful award performance.

If the meeting or conference does not meet this primary purpose test, the costs may be unallowable. The federal award recipient may also have costs for other types of functions that are unallowable.

We will look at several of these loosely related types of costs, specifically:

- Alcoholic beverages
- Entertainment costs
- Fund-raising and investment management costs
- Lobbying costs

Alcoholic Beverages

Alcoholic beverages are unallowable costs to charge the federal award. While alcohol is always an unallowable cost, it may be allowable in research situations required by the federal award; for example, to fuel an alcohol lamp used in a laboratory.

Entertainment

Entertainment costs are usually unallowable and include such items as amusement, diversion, and social activities. However, if the entertainment activity has programmatic value and is authorized in the award budget or pre-approved by the federal awarding agency, the entertainment cost is allowable.

Fund Raising and Investment Management

Fund-raising and investment-management costs are lumped together because of the relationship between fund raising and the need to manage the funds once received.

Fund raising includes organized activities dedicated to raising capital or obtaining contributions. Fund-raising costs are generally unallowable. However, if the purpose of the fund raising is to extend the federal program objectives, the fund-raising cost may be allowable with prior approval from the federal awarding agency.

Investment-management costs are defined as the costs for investment counsel and other costs to enhance income from the federal award recipient's investments. Fund-raising and investment-management costs are generally unallowable except when related to investments covering pension, self-insurance, or other funds that include federal participation.

An appropriate share of indirect costs may need to be allocated to fund-raising and investment activities. If the federal award recipient has costs related to fund raising and is not allocating indirect costs to these functions, it may be a good time to review the requirements for indirect cost allocation.

Lobbying

Lobbying costs are broadly defined as attempts to improperly influence, or to assist another organization in improperly influencing:

- A federal, state, or local government employee or public official to take regulatory action on any basis other than the merits of the matter
- The introduction, enactment, or modification of federal or state legislation

Lobbying costs are unallowable for charging to a federal award. This unallowability extends to a wide range of activities, and includes:

- Soliciting contributions and endorsements
- Preparing, distributing, or using publicity or propaganda

- Urging the members of the general public to participate in any mass demonstration, march, rally, fund-raising drive, lobbying, telephone campaigns, or letter writing

There are extensive restrictions and disclosure requirements on lobbying. However, some lobbying costs may be allowable, such as costs related to providing a technical or factual presentation of information on a topic directly related to the performance of the award. Note that the presentation of information must be in response to a documented request.

Unallowable Advertising, Public Relations, and Marketing

In the next part, we look at costs related to:

- Advertising
- Public relations
- Selling and marketing

Advertising Costs

Advertising costs are defined as costs for advertising media and related administrative activities. Advertising costs can include print media, electronic media, radio and television advertising, and direct mail. Most advertising costs are unallowable to charge to a federal award. There are a few specific exceptions; for example, when the federal award recipient requires advertising to perform the activities of the award. In general, if the advertising is designed solely to promote the federal award recipient, the costs are unallowable.

Public Relations Costs

Public relations costs are defined as costs for community relations and activities to maintain the image of the federal award recipient. This description also includes activities to promote understanding and favorable relations with the public. Public relations costs, such as meetings, conventions, or other events to promote the non-award activities of the federal award recipient, are unallowable.

Other unallowable public relations costs include:

- Displays, exhibits, meeting rooms, and hospitality suites
- Staff compensation to support the unallowable activities
- Promotional items such as memorabilia, gifts, and souvenirs

Selling and Marketing Costs

Selling and marketing costs are generally unallowable when related to any services or products of the federal award recipient. If the awarding agency determines, however, that the selling and marketing costs are necessary to the performance of the award, the costs may be allowed.

Unallowable Legal and Insurance Costs

In this part, we will look at several areas related to legal and insurance costs of the federal award recipient, specifically:

- Defense and prosecution costs
- Fines and penalties
- Insurance costs

Defense and Prosecution Costs

Defense and prosecution costs are defined as the costs related to criminal and civil proceedings, claims, appeals, and patent infringement defense or prosecution. These costs can include legal fees, consulting services, and the clerical staff and expenses to support the legal team.

Defense and prosecution costs have very specific rules related to allowability. In general, defense and prosecution costs are unallowable unless:

- The federal award recipient wins
- The federal award recipient enters into a settlement agreement that provides for the allowability of defense and prosecution costs
- The federal award recipient gets specific written directions to proceed from an authorized official federal awarding agency

Fines and Penalties

Costs resulting from violations of or failures to comply with federal, state, or local laws and regulations are generally unallowable costs. The two exceptions to this unallowability are:

- When the costs arise from complying with specific provisions of an award
- The federal award recipient has received written instructions from the federal awarding agency

Insurance Costs

The definition of insurance costs includes costs for insurance required by the award or insurance carried as part of the general conduct of operations. For the purpose of this regulation, the definition does not include insurance covered under the definition of fringe benefits, such as employee health insurance.

While most types of insurance costs are allowable when consistent with sound business practices, certain types of insurance are unallowable to charge a federal award, namely:

- Insurance covering risk of loss or damage to federal property, unless the federal awarding agency specifically requests or approves such costs

- Management fee coverage in business interruption insurance

- Life insurance for trustees, officers, and similar employees when the federal award recipient is named beneficiary

- Insurance for defects in the federal award recipient's materials or workmanship

- Medical malpractice insurance, in certain circumstances

The federal award recipient should also not charge the federal award for actual losses incurred that could have been covered under allowable insurance.

Note that minor losses for such things as breakage or nominal deductibles on insurance policies are generally allowable.

Other Types of Unallowable Costs

In this part, we will look at the other types of unallowable costs:

- Donations and contributions
- Pre-agreement costs
- Losses on sponsored agreements
- Organizational costs
- General government costs
- Student and activity costs
- Interest costs

Donations

Donations and contributions are defined as donated cash, property, or services and donated goods or space. Donations made by the federal award recipient are unallowable, regardless of where they are donated. Likewise, donations made to the federal award recipient are not reimbursable by the federal award and are therefore also unallowable costs. Note that though unallowable to the federal award, the value of donations received by the federal award recipient, such as donated labor or materials, may be used in calculating cost share under certain circumstances.

Pre-agreement Costs

Pre-agreement costs are defined as costs directly related to and incurred prior to the effective date of the federally sponsored agreement. Pre-agreement costs are also known as pre-award costs. Pre-agreement costs are unallowable, even if costs incurred would have been allowable if incurred during the period of the federally sponsored agreement. However, in some cases an institution may receive the written approval of the sponsoring agency for pre-agreement costs that would be allowable.

Note that federal administrative requirements specifically state that pre-spending on a sponsored agreement is at the institution's risk. The federal government is not under any obligation to pay pre-agreement costs if the institution does not receive the sponsored agreement or receives an amount that is less than expected.

Loss on a Sponsored Agreement

Loss on a sponsored agreement is unallowable. A loss on a sponsored agreement is defined as any excess of costs incurred over the amount of the award. On a related note, it is also prohibited to transfer costs from one award to another just to get around the loss incurred on a sponsored agreement.

Organization Costs

Organization costs include costs for the establishment or reorganization of the organization. The costs may include incorporation fees, attorney, consultant, and investment counselor fees. Organization costs are unallowable to charge a federal award unless the prior approval of the awarding agency is obtained.

Government Costs

General costs of the governmental unit are unallowable. The unallowability extends to governmental services normally provided to the general public, such as costs for fire and police protection. General government costs are unallowable to charge a federal award unless the costs are specifically provided for as a direct cost under the program statute or federal regulations.

Unallowable general government costs include:

- The salaries and expenses for the office of the governor of the state or chief executive of a political subdivision such as a city or a federally recognized tribal government
- Also unallowable are costs for the state legislature, tribal council, and other local governmental bodies such as county boards or city councils

The restriction on general government costs also includes the unallowability of costs for the judiciary branch of government and expenditures on prosecutorial activities. There is an exception to this restriction when government costs are treated as direct costs and are specifically authorized by program statute or federal regulations.

Another exception to unallowability of general government costs is for tribal governments. In this case, the portion of the salaries and expenses for tribal governments directly attributable to managing and operating federal programs are allowable.

Student and Alumni Activity Costs

Student activity costs are generally unallowable to charge to a sponsored agreement unless specifically provided for in the sponsored agreement. Unallowable costs include items such as intramural activities, student publications, student clubs, and related activities.

Costs in support of alumni or alumnae activities and similar services are also unallowable.

Interest Costs

Interest costs are defined as costs incurred for borrowed capital or temporary use of the federal award recipient's funds. Interest costs are divided into two categories:

• Interest on debt to acquire capital assets such as equipment and buildings
• All other interest

Interest costs are generally unallowable unless the costs are related to acquiring or replacing capital assets such as equipment. The rules regarding interest are very specific, so for further details, please refer to the details in 2 CFR Part 200.

 **Key Concepts**

• Many examples of unallowable costs appear in the 2 CFR Part 200.

• These items have very specific rules regarding unallowability of costs. The federal award recipient needs to understand the restrictions so that costs can be properly classified.

Index

About The Author

Lucy Morgan, CPA

Lucy Morgan, CPA is an advocate for federal grant recipients, GPA-approved trainer, CPA, and founding member of My Fed Trainer, LLC, dedicated to making people and organizations more valuable. She has traveled extensively throughout the world, including sailing a 26-foot sailboat from the Western shore of Lake Superior to South Florida via the Great Lakes and the East Coast of the United States. She lives with her sailing partner and husband of more than 30 years in Loveland, Colorado.

More About
Grant Management

If you enjoyed Decoding Grant Management, Lucy Morgan CPA is the ideal speaker and trainer for your next event.

Lucy is a CPA, MBA who has made it her mission to bring a message of how to make people and organizations more valuable.

As an author, speaker, and trainer, she brings over twenty-five years of practical experience, insights, and wisdom with easy-to-understand examples and concepts to a variety of venues.

If you would like to know more about booking Lucy for a keynote, breakout, or workshop, please call My Fed Trainer at 970-744-3214 or e-mail your questions to Support@ MyFedTrainer.com.

Other Books by the Author

Decoding Internet Marketing. 10 Minute Media, Loveland, Colorado, 2013

The Diamond Mindset. 10 Minute Media, Loveland, Colorado, 2015

Notes:

What are your "aha" moments from *Decoding Grant Management?*

_____

_____

_____

_____

_____

_____

_____

_____

_____

_____

_____

_____

_____

See more resources at www.MyFedTrainer.com.